Socialism on Trial

JAMES P. CANNON

Socialism on Trial

EXPANDED TO INCLUDE
DEFENSE POLICY IN THE MINNEAPOLIS TRIAL:
A CRITICISM BY GRANDIZO MUNIS
AND AN ANSWER BY JAMES P. CANNON

PATHFINDER

New York London Montreal Sydney

"Socialism on Trial" was first published by Pioneer Publishers in 1942. "Defense Policy in the Minneapolis Trial" was published in 1942 by Pioneer Publishers. In 1969, Merit Publishers reprinted it with the title "What Policy for Revolutionists—Marxism or Ultra-Leftism?"

ISBN 0-87348-317-0
Library of Congress Catalog Card Number 73-86630

Manufactured in the United States of America

Fifth edition, 1973
Ninth printing, 2001

Pathfinder

410 West Street, New York, NY 10014, U.S.A.
Fax: (212) 727-0150
E-mail: pathfinderpress@compuserve.com

PATHFINDER DISTRIBUTORS AROUND THE WORLD:

Australia (and Asia and the Pacific):
    Pathfinder, 176 Redfern St., 1st floor, Redfern, NSW 2016
    Postal address: P.O. Box K879, Haymarket, NSW 1240
Canada:
    Pathfinder, 2761 Dundas St. West, Toronto, ON, M6P 1Y4
Iceland:
    Pathfinder, Klapparstíg 26, 2d floor, 101 Reykjavík
    Postal address: P. Box 0233, IS 121 Reykjavík
New Zealand:
    Pathfinder, La Gonda Arcade, 203 Karangahape Road, Auckland
    Postal address: P.O. Box 8730, Auckland
Sweden:
    Pathfinder, Vikingagatan 10, S-113 42, Stockholm
United Kingdom (and Europe, Africa except South Africa, and Middle East):
    Pathfinder, 47 The Cut, London, SE1 8LL
United States (and Caribbean, Latin America, and South Africa):
    Pathfinder, 410 West Street, New York, NY 10014

Contents

Next class 03-28-05 pg. 103

Appendix: Defense Policy in the Minneapolis Trial

Minneapolis, 1943. The first victims of the Smith Act surrendering themselves to U.S marshall to begin serving their prison terms.

Other books by James P. Cannon

The First Ten Years of American Communism
The History of American Trotskyism
The Struggle for a Proletarian Party
Notebook of an Agitator
Letters from Prison
Speeches for Socialism
Speeches to the Party

Introduction

Socialism on Trial contains the verbatim testimony of James P. Cannon, then the national secretary of the Socialist Workers Party, in the 1941 trial of twenty-eight prominent members of that party and of Minneapolis Teamsters Local 544. Eighteen were convicted and served twelve- to eighteen-month sentences in prison during 1944–45.

The Minneapolis case was the first peacetime federal prosecution for sedition in American history and the first under the notorious Smith "Gag" Act. It was engineered by the Roosevelt administration as part of its war preparations.

Cannon gave his testimony more than a quarter of a century ago. Yet it remains highly relevant today. In defending the Socialist Workers Party against the federal prosecutors, he had to offer a comprehensive exposition of Marxist strategy and tactics in the struggle against imperialist war.

The wars waged in this century by great powers like the United States, Cannon explained, result from the otherwise insoluble contradictions of capitalism and are utterly reactionary in their nature and objectives. Despite the deceitful slogans of the official propagandists, these wars are not conducted for the preservation of "democracy," "freedom," or any worthy purposes, but for the profit and aggrandizement of the big business interests which have the deciding voice in shaping foreign affairs. That is why "our party is unalterably opposed to all imperialist wars."

The U.S. government, unlike the Soviet Union and China, participated in the Second World War to promote the strategy of the ruling rich to secure world domination for American capitalism. Its subsequent military interventions in Korea, Vietnam, and the Dominican Republic have been no less imperialistic in motivation. But the character of Washington's adversaries has changed.

The main enemy in the Second World War, as in the first, was a rival coalition of imperialist powers; the object of U. S. aggression in the decades since has invariably been a colonial

11

people fighting for its national independence and social emancipation. In such cases revolutionary socialists side with the oppressed nation against its would-be subjugator.

In time of war Marxists are duty bound to articulate the antiwar sentiments of the people, propose a program of effective mass action against the imperialists, and help organize those forces which can bring the reactionary war to an end. Their ultimate aim is to replace the rule of the monopolists and militarists with a socialist government which will have no need to engage in costly and catastrophic foreign adventures.

The Socialist Workers Party opposes capitalist conscription and works for its abolition. Unlike the pacifists and others, however, it does not favor individual resistance to military service for reasons of conscientious objection. Rather than incurring the penalties and isolation resulting from such actions, it is more realistic and effective for drafted opponents of imperialism to go into the armed forces with their fellow conscripts just as workers opposed to capitalism work in the factories of their exploiters.

While on active duty in the army, conscript soldiers need not surrender any of their constitutional liberties but should reserve and exercise the right to think and speak according to their convictions. As Cannon observed: "We think they [the draftees] should have all the rights of citizens. They should have the right to petition Congress; they should have the right to vote; they should have the right to elect committees to present their grievances; they should have the right to elect their own officers, at least the minor officers, and in general they should have the democratic rights of citizens, and we advocate that."

The Socialist Workers Party followed this line during the Vietnam war. Thus Fred Halstead, its presidential candidate in the 1968 campaign, addressed an open letter to GIs which said: "No one has a better right to oppose the war than a combat GI. And while I understand that GIs are in a tight spot, I also know that there is no law that says GIs have to be brainwashed, or that they do not have the right to think for themselves, or to read different points of view on the war, or discuss the war."

The antiwar sentiment within the army, manifested by the GI participants in protest demonstrations, testified to the soundness of this policy in mobilizing joint civilian and GI resistance to the imperialist war-makers.

The circumstances that brought about the celebrated Minneapolis trial provide a clear-cut case of collusion between union bureaucrats and the highest government officials in framing up their opponents. In the spring of 1941 Daniel J. Tobin, head of the Teamsters International and of the Democratic Party Labor Committee, came into headlong conflict with Local 544. That union had been the spearhead of labor organization in the entire Northwest. Its leaders refused to abandon their vigorous struggle to improve working conditions and refused to give political support to Roosevelt's policies in the rapidly approaching entry of the United States into World War II.

After Tobin moved to appoint a receiver with absolute powers over the union, its 4,000 members voted on June 9, 1941, to disaffiliate from Tobin's AFL organization and accept a charter from the CIO. Four days later Roosevelt's secretary, Stephen Early, announced at a White House press conference, as reported in the *New York Times* of June 14, 1941, that Tobin had complained to Roosevelt by telegram and that: "when I advised the President of Tobin's representations this morning he asked me to immediately have the government departments and agencies interested in the matter notified. . . ."

Thirteen days later FBI agents raided the branch offices of the Socialist Workers Party in St. Paul and Minneapolis, carting off large quantities of socialist literature, much of which could have been purchased in bookstores or obtained in any public library. On July 15 a federal grand jury handed down an indictment.

In addition to granting a personal favor to his union supporter Tobin, the president, anticipating direct participation of the United States in the coming war, wished to isolate and silence the advocates of socialism so that their views might be prevented from gaining a hearing.

Toward this end his Department of Justice invoked for the first time the Smith Act passed in 1940. The sponsor of this ultrareactionary legislation was poll-tax Representative Howard W. Smith of Virginia, leader of the antilabor bloc in Congress. This was the first statute since the Alien & Sedition Acts of 1798 to make mere advocacy of ideas a federal crime. The AFL and CIO opposed its enactment and the American Civil Liberties Union pleaded with Roosevelt to veto the law because it violated the Bill of Rights. But the president affixed his signature to it.

Count 1 of the indictment, based on an 1861 statute passed during the Civil War against the Southern slaveholders, alleged a "conspiracy to overthrow the government by force and violence."

Count 2 of the indictment, based wholly on the Smith Act, charged: (1) Advocating overthrow of the government by force; (2) Publishing and circulating literature advocating this; (3) Forming organizations "to teach, advocate and encourage" such overthrow; (4) Becoming members of such organizations; (5) Distributing publications which "advised, counseled and urged" insubordination in the armed forces.

The trial began October 27, 1941, in the Federal District Court at Minneapolis. The principal government "evidence" consisted of innumerable quotations from articles in the American Trotskyist press going back to 1929. Public writings, public addresses of the defendants, radio speeches, leaflets distributed by tens of thousands—these were the main proofs of "conspiracy."

The government further introduced as evidence photographs of the great teachers of Marxism. It introduced leaflets such as the one advertising a public talk by Vincent R. Dunne on how the Socialist Workers Party had mobilized 50,000 antifascists in New York on February 20, 1939, to combat a rally of the Nazi German-American Bund in Madison Square Garden. The indictment and prosecution flatly characterized as criminal the doctrines of Marx, Engels, Lenin, and Trotsky.

This attack was met unflinchingly by the defendants. In no labor trial in this country have defendants so consciously and systematically defended their revolutionary doctrine, utilizing the courtroom as a forum from which to proclaim their real views. The conduct of the defendants at the trial and throughout the case belongs to the best traditions of international socialism.

The jury returned a verdict of "not guilty" on the first count of the indictment, thereby revealing the flimsiness of the government's case. On the second count eighteen defendants were found guilty. They were sentenced on December 8, 1941, the day war was declared against Japan.

The Civil Rights Defense Committee, organized to handle this case, carried the appeal through the Eighth Circuit Court, which sustained the convictions, up to the U. S. Supreme Court. The highest court three times refused to hear the petition of the eighteen.

Here was a manifestly unconstitutional law clearly abrogating the right of free speech. The case was the first to be tried under this law. The president, who appointed the judges, was waging the war ostensibly to make the world safe for democracy. The law had been widely denounced—even in the halls of Congress—as "enough to make Thomas Jefferson turn over in his grave" and as "without precedent in the history of labor legislation." Yet without explanation the final court of appeals rejected the request of the defendants to review and reverse their convictions.

The flagrant injustice of their imprisonment aroused considerable indignation. The American Civil Liberties Union declared: "This is a case which should never have been brought to court under a law which should never have been passed. Never before has the Supreme Court refused to review a case of this importance."

Recognizing the vital importance of the Minneapolis case to the cause of civil liberties and labor's rights, almost 150 international and local unions, representing over five million workers, supported the work of the Civil Rights Defense Committee and its effort to obtain presidential pardon for the eighteen. But they were forced to serve their full sentences.

Among the applauders of the government prosecution of the eighteen were prominent spokesmen for the Communist Party. Blinded by hatred of their Trotskyist political opponents and their unrestrained backing of the imperialist war effort, the Stalinist leaders failed to heed James P. Cannon's warning in the Minneapolis courtroom that the precedent set by the prosecution of the SWP members in Minneapolis could and would be later directed against others. That came to pass when the shifting international strategic interests of the capitalist rulers changed the wartime alliance between the United States and the Soviet Union into hostility and the cold war began. From 1949 on, scores of U. S. Communist Party leaders were sentenced to harsh prison terms under the Smith Act.

Communist Party spokesmen have recently recognized the grievous error of their refusal to protest the victimization of the Socialist Workers Party members. The lesson of their misconduct remains as a warning to others, especially to those liberals and union leaders who, out of anti-Communist prejudices and commitment to cold war policies, have in turn failed to fight the government attacks upon the civil liberties of the Communists. Such disunity undermines the defense of democracy and emboldens the witch-hunters and forces of reaction to further aggressions. The old solidarity slogan, "An injury to one is an injury to all," remains the best guiding line for maintaining civil liberties.

Too many Americans are inclined to rely on "liberal" officials to protect constitutional and civil rights. An antidote to such overtrustfulness is given in the testimony supplied by Francis Biddle who, as solicitor general, authorized this first application of the Smith Act. In his autobiography, published twenty years after the event, Biddle wrote: "History showed that sedition statutes—laws addressed to what men said—invariably have been used to prevent and punish criticism of the government, particularly in time of war. I believe them to be unnecessary and harmful. This particular law made it criminal to advocate destruction of the government by force and violence. I doubted whether any speech or writing should be made criminal. I thought that this provision might be declared unconstitutional under the First Amendment of the Constitution, which protected freedom of utterance. And, with some reluctance, I authorized a prosecution so that the law would be tested at the threshold, and taken to the Supreme Court, where it would, I hoped and believed, be knocked out. . . .

"The judgment was sustained on appeal to the Circuit Court of Appeals; but to my surprise the Supreme Court refused to review it. The victory for the government became a defeat for me. The law stood on the books. Uncomfortable about the result, I was not surprised when the American Civil Liberties Union and some of my liberal friends attacked me.

"I have since come to regret that I authorized the prosecution. I should not have tried to test the criminal provisions of the statute in this particular case. . . . There had been no substantial overt acts outside of talk and threats, openly expressed in the time-honored Marxist lingo." (*In Brief Authority,* pp. 151–2)

Biddle was rewarded for his compliance in the Roosevelt-Tobin conspiracy by appointment as U. S. attorney general soon after. His later repentance may testify to the pricking of his conscience. But that was no solace to the seventeen men and one woman who served months in prison, nor was it any substitute for justice.

One of the most enduring and valuable by-products of this celebrated case makes up the main content of this book. It is the official court record of the testimony given by the veteran revolutionist, James P. Cannon, founder of American Trotskyism.

Here is the unrehearsed, unretouched battle between the prosecuting attorney and the chief defendant. Here are the penetrating questions of defense attorney Albert Goldman in his attempts to make plain what the Socialist Workers Party really stands for, despite constant efforts by the prosecution to create obstacles, becloud the issues, trap the defendants.

More important than the dramatic form is the substance of

this presentation. In the course of the questions Cannon ranges over the broad field of Marxist theory and clarifies the revolutionary socialist program that discloses the only way out of the horrors of capitalist rule.

This remarkable document most closely resembles the memorable declarations of Eugene V. Debs, who suffered imprisonment for his socialist convictions during the First World War. *Socialism on Trial* has come to be recognized as the simplest and best introduction to the application of Marxist ideas to the United States.

Cannon's testimony has been translated into several languages and gone through five large printings in English. It has already helped educate two generations of radicals in this country. This new edition should serve to acquaint the oncoming generation of antiwar militants, civil-rights fighters and radical workers with the merits and meaning of the Marxist method and program as the most effective guide in the struggle against the evils of capitalism and for a socialist America.

The second section of this book was an outgrowth of the first. The group indicted under the Smith Act had had considerable experience with victimization by the authorities in political and union struggles. Their chief attorney, Albert Goldman, was one of the defendants. Cannon had been national secretary of the International Labor Defense from its founding in 1925 through 1928 when it engaged in such famous cases as Mooney and Billings and Sacco and Vanzetti.

The defendants had given careful consideration beforehand to the policy they would follow in the Minneapolis courtroom and in the forum of public opinion. They were resolved to make the most effective and vigorous defense of their individual rights, the ideas of the SWP, and of the trade-union democracy imperiled by the prosecution.

After the convictions of the eighteen, their conduct in the trial was impugned by Grandizo Munis, then a member of the Fourth International, who had fought against Franco in the civil war in his native Spain and was at that time an exile in Mexico. Munis attacked the Minneapolis defense policy from an ultraleft standpoint. The full text of his comments is reprinted here as an appendix, along with the extensive reply to them written by Cannon, who was then out on bail while the convictions were being appealed.

Lenin had analyzed the type of criticism advanced by Munis in his well-known work entitled *Left-Wing Communism: An Infantile Disorder.* Cannon's reply to Munis was so much in accord with Lenin's views on this malady that it can be considered as a sequel to Lenin's refutation of ultraleft thinking in the context of the traditions and conditions of the United States in the early nineteen forties.

Cannon dealt with a wide range of problems in the defense field that are as pertinent today as they were over three decades ago. The U. S. government is again passing "conspiracy" laws designed to stifle resistance against war and racism, imprison dissenters, and crush oppositional movements by force and frameup. Cannon discusses how revolutionaries defend themselves against such attacks, inside the courtroom and outside.

Cannon offers many useful observations on tactics in the courtroom—how correct strategy is determined without sacrifice of revolutionary principle; how to protect one's legality; how to turn around the enemy's attack to make revolutionary propaganda; how to select the proper style, rhetoric, and tone of defense; how to distinguish between "maneuvers" which serve principle and those which contradict it; how to answer charges of advocating or conspiring to use violence, etc.

He indicates how a small revolutionary group should relate to the majority of workers and their allies whom the revolutionary minority is seeking to reach and organize. He outlines the Marxist approach to pacifism, conscientious objection, and desertion. He explains why sabotage and individual terrorism cannot be a substitute for mass action. Perhaps the richest and most valuable part of his reply is his use of historical examples and citations to show the necessity for defensive formulations both as a means of winning mass support and as a preparation for revolutionary action.

The lessons drawn in this classic of American Marxism should be indispensable for the education of the new generation of anticapitalist fighters who will face continuing repression as the radicalization deepens and spreads.

George Novack
August 1973

Socialism on Trial

THE OFFICIAL COURT RECORD
OF JAMES P. CANNON'S TESTIMONY
IN THE MINNEAPOLIS "SEDITION" TRIAL

Testimony by James P. Cannon

District Court of the United States,
District of Minnesota, Fourth Division.

Tuesday, November 18, 1941
Afternoon Session

James P. Cannon

was called as a witness on behalf of the defendants,
having been first duly sworn, testified as follows:

Direct Examination by Mr. Goldman:

Q: Will you please state your name for the reporter?

A: James P. Cannon.

Q: Where do you live, Mr. Cannon?

A: New York.

Q: And your present occupation?

A: National secretary of the Socialist Workers Party.

Q: How old are you, Mr. Cannon?

A: Fifty-one.

Q: Where were you born?

A: Rosedale, Kansas.

Q: How long a period is it since you began your career in the Marxist movement, Mr. Cannon?

A: Thirty years.

Q: What organization did you first join that was part of the working-class movement?

A: The IWW, Industrial Workers of the World.

Q: And did you join any other organization subsequent to that one?

A: The Socialist Party.

Q: And after that?

A: In 1919, at the foundation of the Communist Party, I was one of the original members, and a member of the National Committee since 1920.

Q: How long a period did you remain in the Communist Party?

A: Until October 1928.

Q: Now, will you tell the court and jury the extent of your knowledge of Marxian theory?

A: I am familiar with the most important writings of the Marxist teachers—Marx, Engels, Lenin, Trotsky, and the commentators on their works.

Q: Have you ever read any books against the Marxian theory?

A: Yes. In general I am familiar with the literature against Marxism, particularly the most important book.

Q: Which one is the most important book?

A: Hitler's *Mein Kampf.*

Q: Have you ever edited any labor papers, Mr. Cannon?

A: Yes, a number of them. In fact, I have been more or less a working journalist in the movement for about twenty-five years.

Q: Do you recollect the names of any of the papers that you edited?

A: The *Workers' World* in Kansas City. The *Toiler,* published in Cleveland, Ohio. I was at one time editor of the *Militant.* I was editor of the paper called *Labor Action* published in San Francisco, and I have been on the editorial board of numerous other papers and magazines published in the movement.

Q: Have you ever delivered lectures on the theory of socialism and other aspects of the Marxist movement?

A: Yes, I have done that continuously for about thirty years.

Q: Tell us the reasons why you severed your connection with

the Communist Party, Mr. Cannon.

A: Well, at the time of the controversy that developed in the Russian party between Trotsky on the one side, and Stalin and his group on the other, a controversy that touched many of the most fundamental principles of socialism, this controversy gradually became extended in the Communist International, and became the subject of concern in the other parties of the Communist International. I and some others here took a position in support of Trotsky and that led to our expulsion from the Communist Party of the United States.

Q: Can you give us in brief an idea of the nature of the controversy?

A: It began over the question of bureaucracy in the governmental apparatus of the Soviet Union and in the staffs of the party in Russia. Trotsky began a struggle for more democracy in the party, in the government and unions, and the country generally. This struggle against what Trotsky—and I agree with him—characterized as an increasing bureaucratization of the whole regime, this controversy originating over this point, gradually developed in the course of years into fundamental conflicts over virtually all the basic principles of socialist theory and practice.

Q: And as a result of this controversy, the expulsion took place?

A: As a result of that, the expulsion of our group took place here in the United States, as was the case also in Russia.

Q: In what year was that?

A: 1928.

Q: Tell us what happened to the group that was expelled.

A: We organized ourselves as a group and began to publish a paper called the *Militant*.

Q: And give us some idea of the size of that group, Mr. Cannon.

A: Well, there were only three of us to start with. Eventually we got supporters in other cities. Six months later, when we had our first conference, we had about one hundred members in the country.

Q: And subsequent to that, was there any party organized by this group?

A: Yes, this group called itself originally the Communist League of America, and considered itself still a faction of the Communist Party, attempting to get reinstated into the party, with the provision that we would have a right to hold our views and discuss them in the party. This proposal of ours was rejected by the party, so we developed as an independent organization.

In 1934 we came to an agreement with another organization, which had never been connected with the Communist movement, which had grown out of the trade unions. This organization, originally known as the Conference for Progressive Labor Action, took the name of the American Workers Party. In 1934, in the fall of that year, we had a joint convention with them and formed a common organization which we called the Workers Party of the United States.

Q: And how long did this Workers Party exist?

A: From the fall of 1934 until the spring of 1936.

Q: And what happened then?

A: At that time our party joined the Socialist Party as a body. The Socialist Party had had an internal discussion and controversy, which culminated in the last month of 1935 in a split, in the withdrawal of the more conservative elements. The Socialist Party had then issued an invitation for unaffiliated radical individuals and groups to join the Socialist Party.

We accepted the invitation and joined the party in 1936, again with the express provision which we had originally contended for in the Communist Party, that we should have the right to maintain our particular views and to discuss them in the party— that is, when discussion was in order, and we on our part obligated ourselves to observe discipline in the daily work and common action of the party.

Q: How long did your group remain in the Socialist Party?

A: Just about a year.

Q: And what happened then?

A: Well, the Socialist Party began to impose upon us the same kind of bureaucratism that we had suffered from in the Communist Party. There were great questions disturbing the minds of socialists in that period, particularly the problems of the Spanish Civil War.

Q: And that was in what year?

A: That was in the year 1936, but it became very acute in the spring of 1937. We had a definite position on the Spanish question. We studied it attentively and we wanted to make our views known to the other party members. This was permitted for some time, and then the National Executive Committee issued an order prohibiting any further discussion, prohibiting even the adoption of resolutions by branches on the subject, and we revolted against that provision and insisted on our rights.

At the same time, a big dispute arose in New York over the election campaign—this was the second campaign of La Guardia, and the Socialist Party officially decided to support the candidacy of La Guardia. We opposed it on the ground that it was a violation of socialist principles to support the candidate of a capitalist party. La Guardia was a candidate of the Republican and Fusion parties as well as of the Labor Party.

We also insisted on making our views on this question known and this led to the wholesale expulsion of our people.

Q: When was the Socialist Workers Party organized?

A: The last days of December 1937 and the first day or two of January 1938.

Q: Who participated in its organization?

A: The branches of the Socialist Party which had been expelled—these were banded together under a committee of the expelled branches and this committee was instructed by a conference to arrange a convention, prepare it, and the expelled branches of the Socialist Party sent delegates to the foundation convention of the Socialist Workers Party.

Q: Did this committee of the expelled branches publish any paper?

A: Yes, it published a paper following the expulsions, which began in May or June 1937. We published the *Socialist Appeal,* and that became the official organ of the party after the convention. Later, about a year ago, we changed the name back to our original name, the *Militant*.

Q: To the best of your recollection, how many delegates were present at the founding convention of the Socialist Workers Party?

A: I think about a hundred.

Q: And they came from all over the country, did they?

A: Yes, from about thirty cities, I think—twenty-five or thirty cities.

Q: Now, what did that convention do?

A: The most important decisions of the convention were to set up its organization, adopt a Declaration of Principles, and some collateral resolutions on current questions, and elect a National Committee to direct the work of the party on the basis of the Declaration of Principles.

Q: Did it elect some committee to take charge of the party during the interval between conventions?

A: Yes, that is the National Committee.

Q: Now, you say that it adopted a Declaration of Principles. I show you Prosecution's Exhibit 1, being the Declaration of Principles and Constitution of the Socialist Workers Party, and I ask you whether that is the same that was adopted at the Socialist Workers Party convention? (Document handed to witness)

A: Yes, that is it.

Q: Who presented the Declaration of Principles to the convention, do you remember?

A: Yes, it was presented by the Committee, the National Committee of the expelled branches, which had been selected at a previous conference of the group.

Q: What did the convention, the founding convention of the Socialist Workers Party, adopt as the fundamental aim of the party?

Mr. Schweinhaut (Prosecutor): When?

Q: (By Mr. Goldman): At that time, and subsequent to that time, up until the present, when you are sitting in the stand here.

A: I would say that the fundamental aim of the party then and now is to popularize the doctrines of Marxian socialism and to aid and lead in the work of transforming society from a capitalist to a communist basis.

Q: Give us the meaning of the term socialism.

A: Socialism can have two meanings, and usually does among us. That is, socialism is a name applied to a projected new form of society, and it is a name also applied to the movement working in that direction.

Q: What is the nature of that projected society?

A: We visualize a social order that would be based on the common ownership of the means of production, the elimination of private profit in the means of production, the abolition of the wage system, the abolition of the division of society into classes.

Q: With reference to any government for the purpose of instituting such a society, what would you say is the purpose of the Socialist Workers Party?

A: We have set as our aim the establishment of a workers' and farmers' government, in place of the existing government which we term a capitalist government The task of this government would be to arrange and control the transition of society from the basis of capitalism to the basis of socialism.

Q: When you say "capitalist government," what do you mean?

A: We mean a government that arises from a society that is based on the private ownership of the wealth of the country and the means of production by the capitalists, and which in general represents the interests of that class.

Q: And in contradistinction to this government you propose to establish a workers' and farmers' government?

A: Yes, we propose in place of the capitalists' a workers' and farmers' government, which will frankly represent the economic and social interests of the workers and the producing farmers.

Q: Well, what would happen to the capitalists?

A: Under the workers' and farmers' government, the main

task of the government will be to carry out the transfer of the most important means of production from private ownership to the common ownership of the people.

Q: Well, what would happen to the individual capitalists who would lose their wealth?

A: What do you mean, "happen to them," in what way?

Q: Would you kill them or put them to work or what?

A: Well, under our theory, citizenship participation in the benefits of society would be open to everybody on a basis of equality. This would apply to former capitalists as well as to workers and farmers.

Q: When you use the term "productive wealth," do you mean any property that an individual owns?

A: No—when we speak of the means of production, the wealth of the country, we mean that wealth which is necessary for the production of the necessities of the people. The industries, the railroads, mines, and so on. We don't propose—at least, Marxist socialists have never proposed anywhere that I know—the elimination of private property in personal effects. We speak of those things which are necessary for the production of the people's needs. They shall be owned in common by all the people.

Q: What would happen to small businesses, the owners of which do not have labor to hire?

A: Well, the best Marxist authority since Engels is that small proprietors, who are not exploiters, should be in no way interfered with by the workers' and farmers' government. They should be allowed to have their farms, their small possessions, their small handicraft shops, and only insofar as they become convinced, by the example of socialized collective farming and voluntarily would agree to pool their land and their resources in a collective effort, only to that extent can collectivization of small farming enterprises take place.

In the meantime, it is a part of our program that the workers' and farmers' government should assist such enterprise by assuring them reasonable prices for their implements, for fertilizers, arrange credits for them, and in general conduct the government as a government which is concerned for them and wants to represent their interests.

I am speaking now of small producing farmers, not of big landowners and bankers, who exploit a lot of people, or who rent land out to sharecroppers. We certainly intend to socialize *their* land in the very first stages of the workers' and farmers' government, turn it over to the administration of the people who actually till the soil. That also, I may say, is the standard Marxist doctrine since the earliest days, and the doctrine of Lenin and Trotsky in the Russian Revolution.

Q: How will this socialist society be controlled and directed?

A: Well, socialism naturally would have to grow out of the new situation. After the social revolution has been effected in the political arena, and the capitalist government has been replaced by a workers' and farmers' government, which proceeds to the socialization of the industries, the abolition of inequalities, the raising of the level of the income of the masses of the people, and the suppression of any attempts at counterrevolution by the dispossessed exploiters, the importance and weight of the government as a repressive force would gradually diminish.

Then as classes are abolished, as exploitation is eliminated, as the conflict of class against class is eliminated, the very reason for the existence of a government in the strict sense of the term begins to diminish. Governments are primarily instruments of repression of one class against another. According to the doctrine of Marx and Engels and all of the great Marxists who followed them, and based themselves on their doctrine, we visualize, as Engels expressed it, a gradual withering away of the government as a repressive force, as an armed force, and its replacement by purely administrative councils, whose duties will be to plan production, to supervise public works, and education, and things of this sort. As you merge into socialist society, the government, as Engels expressed it, tends to wither away and the government of men will be replaced by the administration of things.

The government of a socialist society in reality will be an

administrative body, because we don't anticipate the need for armies and navies, jails, repressions, and consequently that aspect of government dies out for want of function.

Q: What is the Marxian theory as to the social forces making socialism inevitable?

A: Capitalism is a state of society that did not always exist. Like preceding social systems, it went through a period of gestation in the womb of the old feudal society. It grew and developed as against feudal society, eventually overthrew it by revolutionary means, raised the productivity of mankind to undreamed of heights—

MR. SCHWEINHAUT: Well, now, just a moment, Mr. Cannon. It seems to me this question could be answered much more simply than this. I suspect the gentleman is going to make a speech now, and I don't see that the question calls for it at all.

Q: (By Mr. Goldman): Well, as briefly as you can, describe the social forces—

A: I did not want to make a speech. I wanted to say in a few words what are the social forces that are pushing capitalism to bankruptcy. The laws by which—

MR. SCHWEINHAUT: That was not the question that was asked you, Mr. Witness. You were asked what were the social forces that would make socialism inevitable, or some such thing. Well, I give up. Go ahead.

THE WITNESS: I assure you that I am anxious to compress the explanation as much as possible.

Capitalism operates by certain internal laws which were analyzed and laid bare for the first time by Karl Marx in his great works, first in the *Communist Manifesto* and then in *Capital*.

Now, the two internal laws of capitalism which are making inevitable its decline and its replacement by socialism are these:

One, the private ownership of the means of production and the employment of wage labor at wages less than the value of the product produced by the wage laborer. This creates a surplus which the capitalist proprietor has to sell in the market. It is obvious that the wage worker, who receives for his labor less than the total value of his product, can be a customer only for that amount of the value that he receives in the form of wages. The balance is surplus value, as Marx explained it, for which the capitalist must find a market

The more capitalism expands within a given country, the more productive becomes the labor of the worker, the greater is this surplus, which cannot find a market because the great mass of the people who produce the wealth do not receive enough wages to buy it. And that leads capitalism into periodic crises of what they call overproduction, or as some popular agitators call it underconsumption, but the scientific term is overproduction.

Capitalism from its very inception, for more than a hundred years, pretty nearly two hundred years, has gone through such crises. Now, in the past, capitalism could solve these crises eventually by finding new markets, new fields of investment, new fields of exploitation, and as long as capitalism could find new areas for the investment of capital and the sale of goods, the capitalist system could extricate itself from this cyclical crisis which occurred about every ten years, and go on to new heights of production. But every time capitalism experienced a new boom, and began to develop some new territory, it narrowed down the world. Because every place that capitalism penetrated, its laws followed it like a shadow, and the new field of exploitation began to become also surfeited with a surplus.

For example, the United States, which was a great reservoir for the assimilation of surplus products of Europe and gave European capitalism a breathing spell, has itself developed in the course of one hundred and fifty years to the point where it produces an enormous surplus and has to fight Europe for a market in which to sell it. So this tremendous contradiction between the private ownership of industry and wage labor presents capitalism more and more with an insoluble crisis. This is one law of capitalism.

The second law is the conflict between the development of the productive forces and the national barriers in which they are confined under capitalism. Every country operating on a capitalist basis produces a surplus which it is unable to sell in its domestic market for the reasons I have given you before.

What, then, is the next step? The capitalists must find a foreign market. They must find a foreign market in which to sell their surplus and a foreign field in which to invest their surplus capital. The difficulty confronting capitalism is that the world doesn't get any bigger. It retained the same size, while every modern capitalist nation was developing its productive forces far beyond its own domestic capacity to consume. Or to sell at a profit. This led to the tremendous explosion of the World War in 1914. The World War of 1914 was, in our theory and our doctrine, the signal that the capitalist world had come to a bankrupt crisis.

Q: What would you say about the law of competition working within the capitalist system?

A: The law of competition between capitalists results inevitably in the bigger capitalists, the ones with the more modern, more efficient, and productive enterprises, crushing out the small ones, either by destroying them or absorbing them until the number of independent proprietors grows continually less and the number of pauperized people increases by leaps and bounds, until the wealth becomes concentrated in the hands of a very few people, and the great mass of the people, especially of the workers, are confronted with ever-increasing difficulties of an economic and social nature.

I mentioned the World War of 1914 as the signal that capitalism on the world scale wasn't able to solve any of its problems peacefully before. They had to kill eleven million men, and then make a peace and prepare to do it all over again the second time. That, in the view of the Marxian socialists, is the sign that capitalism has outlived its possibility to solve its own problems.

Q: What would you say, then, with reference to the relative importance of the economic factor moving toward socialism, and the agitation for socialism of the various parties, including the Socialist Workers Party?

A: Well, now, if I could just explain here, Marxian socialism is distinct from what is known in our terminology as utopian socialism—that is, the socialism of people who visualize a better form of society, and think that it is only necessary to see that a better society could exist, and to persuade the people to adopt it and solve the problem. Marxian socialism proceeds from the theory that the very internal laws by which capitalism operates drive society to a socialist solution.

I mentioned the war—I mentioned the conflict between the various capitalist nations which are always now in either a state of war, or of an armed truce preparing for war. I should mention also the experience of the 1929 depression, as it is called, with its fifteen million able-bodied American workers who were willing to work unable to find employment. That was another sign of a terrible unhealthiness in the social organism called capitalism; and the unemployment scourge operated on a world scale.

Now, these are the forces that are driving society to a rational solution, in our opinion, by the nationalization of industry, the elimination of competition, and the abolition of private ownership. Our agitation could never effect the transformation of one social order to another unless these powerful internal economic laws were pushing it.

The real revolutionary factors, the real powers that are driving for socialism, are the contradictions within the capitalist system itself. All that our agitation can do is to try to foresee theoretically what is possible and what is probable in the line of social revolution, to prepare people's minds for it, to convince them of the desirability of it, to try to organize them to accelerate it and to bring it about in the most economical and effective way. That is all agitation can do.

Q: What role does the factor of fascism play?

A: Fascism is another sign that unfailingly appears in every capitalist society when it reaches that period of decay and crisis and isn't any longer able to keep an equilibrium of society on the basis of democratic parliamentarism, which has been the governmental form of rule of capitalism in its heyday. Fascism grows, becomes a terrible menace to mankind, and a terrible warning to the workers that if they don't bestir themselves and take things in their own hands, they will suffer the fate for years that has befallen the people of Germany and Italy and other countries now in Europe.

Q: Now, what was the purpose for the adoption of the Declaration of Principles?

A: The general purpose was to put down in written form a clear statement of our principles, to inform the world what our party stood for, and to guide the party in its actions following the convention, to lay down a body of doctrines and ideas which could govern the work of the party and guide its National Committee, in editing its paper, and so forth.

Q: Were there any secret agreements entered into by this committee that formulated the Declaration of Principles, agreements which were not revealed to the convention or to anybody else?

A: No, everything we stand for we put in the Declaration of Principles. We couldn't do it otherwise.

It is impossible to build a political movement on the basis of one program, and expect that it will serve another program. That, I could tell you, is a political law that is known to every serious politician; a political party or a political man is bound by his own slogans. If a party puts forward a slogan or a program—

MR. SCHWEINHAUT: Well, now please, Mr. Cannon. You have answered—

THE COURT: Don't you think this is argumentative?

MR. GOLDMAN: All right!

Q: Now, how long was the Declaration of Principles in effect?

A: From the first week in January 1938, until the last month in 1940.

Q: And what happened in December 1940?

A: A specially called convention of the party adopted a resolution to suspend the Declaration of Principles and to instruct the National Committee to prepare a new draft for the consideration of the party at a subsequent convention or conference.

Q: What were the reasons for this action of the convention?

A: The principal reason, I may say, was the passage by Congress of a law known as the Voorhis Act which penalized parties belonging to international organizations. That was the principal reason.

Subsidiary reasons were that in the meantime the party had changed its position on the question of the labor party. Some questions had become outdated by the passage of events, and in general we felt the necessity of a new draft.

Q: Can you tell us in brief the nature of the change on the labor party?

A: It was a change in the opposite direction. At the time of the adoption of the Declaration, we refused to support these proposals for the organization of a labor party—that is, a party based on the trade unions. By the summer of 1938, we changed our mind about that and came to the conclusion that this movement would have more progressive potentialities than otherwise.

Q: And tell us what the method used was in adopting that change.

A: The National Committee adopted a resolution setting forth its changed position. This resolution then was sent to the party members in the internal bulletin, and a discussion period, I think of sixty days, was opened up in which anybody could express his opinion for or against the change. It was discussed very thoroughly in the party. In fact, not all members of the National Committee agreed with the change. At the end of the discussion period a referendum vote was taken of the membership, and a majority voted in favor of the amended resolution.

Q: What, if anything, was done subsequent to the suspension of this Declaration of Principles with reference to the adoption of a new set of principles?

A: We appointed a committee to make a new draft of a Declaration.

Q: And was that draft made?

A: The draft was made. We held a conference in Chicago

just on the eve of this trial—I think October 10, 11 and 12—
we held a conference of the party in connection with a meeting of the National Committee, where the new draft was submitted and accepted by the conference, for submission to the
party for discussion and possible amendment.

Q: (By Mr. Goldman): Does the Declaration of Principles that
was originally adopted, and subsequently suspended, teach the
necessity of social revolution, Mr. Cannon?

A: Yes.

Q: What is meant by "social revolution"?

A: By social revolution is meant a transformation, a political
and economic transformation of society.

Q: And the nature of the transformation is what?

A: Is fundamental and affects the property system, affects
the method of production.

Q: Is there a distinction between political and social revolution?

A: Yes.

Q: What is the distinction?

A: Well, a *political* revolution can occur without any radical
transformation of the underlying economic structure of society, the property basis of society.
A *social* revolution, on the other hand, affects not only the
government, but affects the economic system.

Q: Can you give us any examples of both the social and political revolutions?

A: Yes. The great French Revolution of 1789—

MR. SCHWEINHAUT: Was that a political or social revolution? ·

THE WITNESS: That was a social revolution, because it transformed the property basis of society from feudal property to
capitalist property.

Q: (By Mr. Goldman): What do you mean by "feudal property"?

A: That was the whole economic system of society that was
based on rights and privileges and restrictions, and serfdom, and
so forth. Capitalist private property, which transformed the farms
into privately owned enterprises of individual farmers, elimi-

nated entirely all vestiges of serfdom and substituted wage labor, made a fundamental change in the economy of France.

Q: And can you give us an example of a political revolution?

A: Two of them occurred in France subsequent to the great social revolution, they occurred in 1830 and 1848—that is, revolutions which were designed merely to change the ruling bureaucracy of the country and without touching the property system.

A revolution such as occurred in Panama the other day, a simple replacement of one regime by another in a palace coup d'etat, that is a political revolution that doesn't affect the economic character of society at all.

We consider the American Civil War was a social revolution because it destroyed the system of slave labor and property in slaves, and replaced it by the complete domination of capitalist enterprise and wage labor.

Q: Enumerate the conditions under which, according to Marxist theory, the social revolution against capitalism will occur.

A: I can give you quite a number.

The first one is that the existing society must have exhausted its possibilities of further development. Marx laid down as a law that no social system can be replaced by another until it has exhausted all its possibilities for development and advancement. That is, you may say, the fundamental prerequisite for a social revolution.

Then I can give a number of collateral prerequisites which have been accepted by our movement.

1. The ruling class must be unable any longer to solve its problems, must have to a large degree lost confidence in itself.

2. The misery and desperation of the masses must have increased to the point where they desire at all costs a radical change. Unemployment, fascism and war become problems of increasing magnitude which are patently insoluble by the existing ruling class. There must be a tremendous sentiment among the masses of the producers for socialist ideas and for a socialist revolution.

And, in addition to these prerequisites I have mentioned, it is necessary to have a workers' party that is capable of leading and organizing the movement of the workers in a resolute fashion for a revolutionary solution of the crisis.

Q: Now, what would you say as to the actual existence at the present time of the factor of the decline of capitalism and the fact that it has exhausted the possibilities of further growth at the present moment, as far as the United States is concerned?

A: Taken on a world scale, capitalism had exhausted its possibilities of further development by 1914. On a world scale, capitalism has never since that time attained the level of productivity of 1914. On the other hand, America, which is the strongest section of world capitalism, experienced an enormous boom in the same period when capitalism as a world system was declining. But American capitalism, as was shown by the 1929 crisis, and now by the war preparations, has also definitely entered into the stage of decay.

Q: And what are the symptoms of that decay?

A: The symptoms were the army of fifteen million unemployed, the decline of production from 1929; the fact that the higher productive index of the present day is based almost entirely on armament production, which is no possible basis of permanent stability.

Q: What would you say as to the existence at the present time of the second factor that you enumerated as a prerequisite to a revolutionary situation, namely, the inability of the ruling class to solve their problems?

A: I do not think it has by any means yet reached the acute stage in this country that it must necessarily reach on the eve of a revolution. They can't solve their problems here, but they don't know it yet.

MR. ANDERSON: (Prosecutor): What was the last of that answer, Mr. Reporter?

THE WITNESS: I say, the American ruling class cannot solve its problems, but is not yet aware of it.

MR. ANDERSON: I see.

THE WITNESS: I didn't mean that as a wisecrack, because as I stated previously, the ruling class must lose confidence in itself, as was the case in every country where a revolution occurred.

Q: (By Mr. Goldman): What is the position of the party on the attempt of Roosevelt to improve the social system in this country?

A: How do you mean, "improve the social system"?

Q: To set capitalism into motion again, after the depression of 1929.

A: Well, all these measures of the New Deal were made possible in this country, and not possible for the poorer countries of Europe, because of the enormous accumulation of wealth in this country. But the net result of the whole New Deal experiment was simply the expenditure of billions and billions of dollars to create a fictitious stability, which in the end evaporated.

Now the Roosevelt administration is trying to accomplish the same thing by the artificial means of a war boom; that is, of an armament boom, but again, in our view, this has no possibility of permanent stability at all.

Q: With reference to the misery and suffering of the masses, what would you say as to the existence of that factor in the United States?

A: In our view, the living standards of the masses have progressively deteriorated in this country since 1929. They haven't yet reached that stage which I mentioned as a prerequisite of an enormous upsurge of revolutionary feeling, but millions of American workers were pauperized following 1929; and that, in our opinion, is a definite sign of the development of this prerequisite for the revolution.

Q: Has the party, or any responsible member of the party, made any prediction as to the length of time that it will take before the masses reach a stage of misery and suffering where they will look for a way out by accepting socialism?

MR. SCHWEINHAUT: Just answer that yes or no.

MR. GOLDMAN: You can answer that yes or no and then I can proceed further.

MR. SCHWEINHAUT: Here is what I want to know, whether it was in writing, or verbally, and under what circumstances?

THE WITNESS: I don't recall any prediction in terms of years, but the question has been raised and debated, and different opinions prevail. I can tell you very briefly about that, if you wish.

MR. SCHWEINHAUT: I object to that.

MR. GOLDMAN: The evidence is full, Your Honor, on the side of the government, as to what the defendants said about when the revolution will come, and under what conditions, and I want an authoritative statement from the head of the party.

MR. SCHWEINHAUT: I will withdraw the objection.

THE WITNESS: I don't recall any prediction as to the number of years. We are trained in the historical method, and we think in terms of history.

MR. SCHWEINHAUT: Please answer the question. You said that you don't remember anybody's prediction in terms of years, but it has been debated. Tell us who debated it, and where, instead of what you think about it.

THE WITNESS: All right. Trotsky advanced the thesis in the early days of our movement that America will be the last country to become socialist, and that the whole of Europe, socialist Europe, would have to defend itself against the intervention of American capitalism.

At a later stage, in the time of our 1929 crisis, Trotsky modified his prediction and said it is not by any means assured that America cannot be the first to enter the path of revolution.

Different opinions of that kind have been expressed in our ranks, but there is no settled opinion that I know of—no settled decision.

Q: (By Mr. Goldman): Calling your attention to that factor that you enumerated as a prerequisite for the social revolution here in the United States, namely, the one of acceptance by the majority of the people of the socialist idea, what would you say with reference to that factor at the present time within the United States?

A: Somewhat lacking, I would say.

Q: Well, explain that.

A: The great mass of American people are still unfamiliar with socialist ideas. That is shown in various ways—by our election results, by attendance at our meetings, circulation of our press, and so on. It is shown that a very small percentage of the American people are interested in socialist ideas at the present time.

Q: How many votes did you receive as candidate for mayor in New York?

A: I don't know whether they counted them all or not—

THE COURT: We will have our recess.

(Afternoon Recess)

start here.

THE COURT: Proceed.

Q: (By Mr. Goldman): I call your attention to the condition which you mentioned as a prerequisite for a social revolution in the United States—that is, the one dealing with a party, and ask you whether that exists at the present time in the United States?

A: No, a party sufficiently influential, no, by no means.

Q: What function does the party play prior to the transformation of the social order?

A: Well, the only thing it can do, when it is a minority party, is to try to popularize its ideas, its programs, by publishing papers, magazines, books, pamphlets, holding meetings, working in trade unions—by propaganda and agitation.

Q: Will you tell the court and jury what is meant by "class struggle" as used by Marx?

A: I can't do it in two sentences, of course. Do you refer to the class struggle in present society?

Q: Yes, confine yourself to the class struggle in present society.

A: Marx contended that present day society is divided into two main classes. One is the capitalists, or the bourgeoisie. The bourgeoisie is a French designation which is used by Marx interchangeably with the expression "the modern capitalist."

The other main class is the working class, the proletariat.

These are the two main classes in society. The workers are exploited by the capitalists. There is a constant conflict of interests between them, an unceasing struggle between these classes, which can only culminate in the eventual victory of the proletariat and the establishment of socialism.

Q: Whom would you include under the term "working class"?

A: We use the term working class, or proletariat, to designate the modern wage workers. Frequently it is broadened in its application to include working farmers, sharecroppers, tenant farmers, real dirt farmers, and so on, but that is not a precise, scientific use of the word as Marx defines it.

Q: What other classes, if any, are there outside the working class and the capitalist class, according to Marxian theory?

A: Between these two main powerful classes in society is the class which Marx describes as the petty bourgeoisie—that is, the small proprietors, the small operators, people who have their own little shops, small stores, the farmer who owns a small farm—they constitute a class which Marx called the petty bourgeoisie.

Q: What would you say with reference to the professional classes?

A: Yes, roughly they are included also in this petty-bourgeois category in Marxian terminology.

Q: And what is the attitude of the party towards this middle class?

A: It is the opinion of the party that the wage working class alone cannot successfully achieve the social revolution. The workers must have the support of the decisive majority of the petty bourgeoisie and, in particular, of the small farmers. That, reiterated time and time again by Trotsky on the basis of the Russian and German experiences, is an absolute prerequisite for success in a revolution—that the workers must have the support of the petty bourgeoisie. Otherwise, the fascists will get them, as was the case in Germany, and instead of a progressive social revolution, you get a reactionary counterrevolution of fascism.

Q: Define the term "dictatorship of the proletariat."

A: "Dictatorship of the proletariat" is Marx's definition of the state that will be in operation in the transition period between the overthrow of capitalism and the institution of the socialist society. That is, the workers' and farmers' government will, in the opinion of the Marxists, be a class dictatorship in that it will frankly represent the workers and farmers, and will not even pretend to represent the economic interests of the capitalists.

Q: What form will that dictatorship take with reference to the capitalist class?

A: Well, you mean, what would be the attitude toward the dispossessed capitalists?

Q: Yes, how will it exercise its dictatorship over the capitalist class?

A: That depends on a number of conditions. There is no fixed rule. It depends on a number of conditions, the most important of which is the wealth and resources of the given country where the revolution takes place; and the second is the attitude of the capitalist class, whether the capitalists reconcile themselves to the new regime or take up an armed struggle against it.

Q: What is the difference between the scientific definition of dictatorship of the proletariat and the ordinary use of the word dictatorship?

A: Well, the popular impression of dictatorship is a one-man rule, an absolutism. I think that is the popular understanding of the word dictatorship. This is not contemplated at all in the Marxian term dictatorship of the proletariat. This means the dictatorship of a class.

Q: And how will the dictatorship of the proletariat operate insofar as democratic rights are concerned?

A: We think it will be the most democratic government from the point of view of the great masses of the people that has ever existed, far more democratic, in the real essence of the matter, than the present bourgeois democracy in the United States.

Q: What about freedom of speech and all the freedoms that

we generally associate with democratic government?

A: I think in the United States you can say with absolute certainty that the freedoms of speech, press, assemblage, religion, will be written in the program of the victorious revolution.

Q: Now, what is the opinion of Marxists with reference to the change in the social order, as far as its being accompanied or not accompanied by violence?

A: It is the opinion of all Marxists that it will be accompanied by violence.

Q: Why?

A: That is based, like all Marxist doctrine, on a study of history, the historical experiences of mankind in the numerous changes of society from one form to another, the revolutions which accompanied it, and the resistance which the outlived classes invariably put up against the new order. Their attempt to defend themselves against the new order, or to suppress by violence the movement for the new order, has resulted in every important social transformation up to now being accompanied by violence.

Q: Who, in the opinion of Marxists, initiated that violence?

A: Always the ruling class; always the outlived class that doesn't want to leave the stage when the time has come. They want to hang on to their privileges, to reinforce them by violent measures, against the rising majority and they run up against the mass violence of the new class, which history has ordained shall come to power.

Q: What is the opinion of Marxists, as far as winning a majority of the people to socialist ideas?

A: Yes, that certainly is the aim of the party. That is the aim of the Marxist movement, has been from its inception. Marx said the social revolution of the proletariat—I think I can quote his exact words from memory—"is a movement of the immense majority in the interests of the immense majority." He said this in distinguishing it from previous revolutions which had been made in the interest of minorities, as was the case in France in 1789.

Q: What would you say is the opinion of Marxists as far as

the desirability of a peaceful transition is concerned?

A: The position of the Marxists is that the most economical and preferable, the most desirable method of social transformation, by all means, is to have it done peacefully.

Q: And in the opinion of the Marxists, is that absolutely excluded?

A: Well, I wouldn't say absolutely excluded. We say that the lessons of history don't show any important examples in favor of the idea so that you can count upon it.

Q: Can you give us examples in American history of a minority refusing to submit to a majority?

A: I can give you a very important one. The conception of the Marxists is that, even if the transfer of political power from the capitalists to the proletariat is accomplished peacefully—then the minority, the exploiting capitalist class, will revolt against the new regime, no matter how legally it is established.

I can give you an example in American history. The American Civil War resulted from the fact that the Southern slaveholders couldn't reconcile themselves to the legal parliamentary victory of Northern capitalism, the election of President Lincoln.

Q: Can you give us an example outside of America where a reactionary minority revolted against a majority in office?

A: Yes, in Spain—the coalition of workers' and liberal parties in Spain got an absolute majority in the elections and established the People's Front government. This government was no sooner installed than it was confronted with an armed rebellion, led by the reactionary capitalists of Spain.

Q: Then the theory of Marxists and the theory of the Socialist Workers Party, as far as violence is concerned, is a prediction based upon a study of history, is that right?

A: Well, that is part of it. It is a prediction that the outlived class, which is put in a minority by the revolutionary growth in the country, will try by violent means to hold on to its privileges against the will of the majority. That is what we predict.

Of course, we don't limit ourselves simply to that prediction. We go further, and advise the workers to bear this in mind and prepare themselves not to permit the reactionary outlived minority to frustrate the will of the majority.

Q: What role does the rise and existence of fascism play with reference to the possibility of violence?

A: That is really the nub of the whole question, because the reactionary violence of the capitalist class, expressed through fascism, is invoked against the workers. Long before the revolutionary movement of the workers gains the majority, fascist gangs are organized and subsidized by millions in funds from the biggest industrialists and financiers, as the example of Germany showed—and these fascist gangs undertake to break up the labor movement by force. They raid the halls, assassinate the leaders, break up the meetings, burn the printing plants, and destroy the possibility of functioning long before the labor movement has taken the road of revolution.

I say that is the nub of the whole question of violence. If the workers don't recognize that, and do not begin to defend themselves against the fascists, they will never be given the possibility of voting on the question of revolution. They will face the fate of the German and Italian proletariat and they will be in the chains of fascist slavery before they have a chance of any kind of a fair vote on whether they want socialism or not.

It is a life and death question for the workers that they organize themselves to prevent fascism, the fascist gangs, from breaking up the workers' organizations, and not to wait until it is too late. That is in the program of our party.

Q: What difference is there, Mr. Cannon, between advocating violence and predicting violent revolution?

MR. SCHWEINHAUT: I object to that.

THE COURT: Is this man qualified to answer that question? Is that a question for him to answer?

MR. SCHWEINHAUT: It is for the jury to determine.

MR. GOLDMAN: I will rephrase the question.

Q: (By Mr. Goldman): What is the attitude of the Socialist Workers Party as far as advocating violent revolution is concerned?

A: No, so far as I know, there is no authority among the most representative teachers of Marxism for advocating violent revolution. If we can have the possibility of peaceful revolution by the registration of the will of the majority of the people, it seems to me it would be utterly absurd to reject that, because if we don't have the support of the majority of the people, we can't make a successful revolution anyhow.

Q: Explain the sentence that I read from page 6 of the Declaration of Principles, Government's Exhibit 1:

*"The belief that in such a country as the United States we live in a free democratic society in which fundamental economic change can be effected by persuasion, by education, by legal and purely parliamentary method, is an illusion."

A: That goes back to what I said before, that we consider it an illusion for the workers to think that the ruling-class violence will not be invoked against them in the course of their efforts to organize the majority of the people.

Q: What is meant by the expression "overthrow of the capitalist state"?

A: That means to replace it by a workers' and farmers' government; that is what we mean.

Q: What is meant by the expression "destroy the machinery of the capitalist state"?

A: By that we mean that when we set up the workers' and farmers' government in this country, the functioning of this government, its tasks, its whole nature, will be so profoundly and radically different from the functions, tasks, and nature of the bourgeois state, that we will have to replace it all along the line. From the very beginning the workers' state has a different foundation and it is different in all respects. It has to create an entirely new apparatus, a new state apparatus from top to bottom. That is what we mean.

Q: Do you mean that there will be no Congress or House of Representatives and Senate?

A: It will be a different kind of a Congress. It will be a Congress of representatives of workers and soldiers and farmers, based on their occupational units, rather than the present form based on territorial representation.

Q: And what is the meaning of "soviet"?

A: Soviet is a Russian word which means "council." It is the Russian equivalent for council in our language. It means a body of representatives of various groups. That is what the term meant in the Russian Revolution. That is, the representatives—they called them deputies—I guess we would call them delegates. The delegates from various shops in a given city come together in a central body. The Russians called it the Soviet of Workers' and Soldiers' Deputies.

Q: Now, what is meant by "expropriation"?

A: Expropriation we apply to big industry, which is in the hands of private capitalists, the Sixty Families—take it out of their hands and put it in the hands of the people through their representatives, that's expropriation.

Q: Is it a question of principle that there should be no compensation for property expropriated from the Sixty Families?

A: No, it is not a question of principle. That question has been debated interminably in the Marxist movement. No place has any authoritative Marxist declared it a question of principle not to compensate. It is a question of possibility, of adequate finances, of an agreement of the private owners to submit, and so forth.

Q: Would the party gladly pay these owners if they could avoid violence?

A: I can only give you my opinion.

Q: What is your opinion?

A: My personal opinion is that if the workers reached the point of the majority, and confronted the capitalist private owners of industry with the fact of their majority and their power, and then we were able to make a deal with the capitalists to compensate them for their holdings, and let them enjoy this for the rest of their lives, I think it would be a cheaper, a cheaper and more satisfactory way of effecting the necessary social transformation than a civil war. I personally would vote for it—if you could get the capitalists to agree on that, which you couldn't.

✳ finish here.

Q: What attitude does the party take toward the ballot?

A: Our party runs candidates wherever it is able to get on the ballot. We conduct very energetic campaigns during the elections, and in general, to the best of our ability, and to the limit of our resources, we participate in election campaigns.

Q: What campaigns do you remember the party having participated in the last few years?

A: Well, I remember the candidacy of Comrade Grace Carlson for the United States Senate last year. I have been a candidate of the party several times for various offices. In Newark, where we have a good organization, we have had candidates in every election for some time. I cite those three examples. In general, it is the policy of the party to have candidates everywhere possible.

Q: Does the party at times support other candidates?

A: Yes. In cases where we don't have a candidate, it is our policy, as a rule, to support the candidates of another workers' party, or of a labor or a farmer-labor party. We support them critically. That is, we do not endorse their program, but we vote for them and solicit votes for them, with the explanation that we don't agree with their program. We support them as against the candidates of the Republican and Democratic parties.

For example, we have always supported the Farmer-Labor candidates in Minnesota in all cases where we didn't have a candidate of our own party. We supported the candidates of the American Labor Party in New York in similar circumstances.

Q: What is the purpose of the party in participating in these electoral campaigns?

A: The first purpose, I would say, is to make full use of the democratic possibility afforded to popularize our ideas, to try to get elected wherever possible; and, from a long range view, to test out the uttermost possibility of advancing the socialist cause by democratic means.

Q: What purpose did you and associates of yours have in creating the Socialist Workers Party?

A: The purpose was to organize our forces for the more effective propagation of our ideas, with the ultimate object that

I have mentioned before, of building up a party that would be able to lead the working masses of the country to socialism by means of the social revolution.

Q: What is the attitude of the party, and the opinion of the party, with reference to the government, as it exists now, being capitalist?

A: Yes, we consider it a capitalist government. That is stated in our Declaration of Principles; that is, a government which represents the economic interests of the class of capitalists in this country, and not the interests of the workers and the poor farmers; not the interests of all the people, as it pretends, but a class government.

Q: What opinion has the party as to differences within the ruling class from the point of view of more liberal or more reactionary?

A: We don't picture the capitalist class as one solid, homogeneous unit. There are all kinds of different trends, different interests among them, which reflect themselves in different capitalist parties and different factions in the parties, and very heated struggles. An example is the present struggle between the interventionists and the isolationists.

Q: Does the party take an attitude as to whether or not the Roosevelt administration is more or less liberal than previous administrations?

MR. SCHWEINHAUT: I object to that as irrelevant.

THE COURT: Sustained.

Q: Is it possible for a difference of opinion to exist in the party on the question as to whether the transformation will be peaceful or violent?

A: I think it is possible, yes.

Q: So that there is no compulsion on a member to have an opinion as to what the future will have in store for the party or for the workers?

A: No, I don't think that is compulsory, because that is an opinion about the future that can't be determined with scientific precision.

Q: What steps, if any, does the party take to secure a correct interpretation of party policy by individual members?

A: Well, we have, in addition to our public lectures, and press, forums, and so forth—we have internal meetings, educational meetings. In the larger cities we usually conduct a school, where we teach the doctrines of the party. Individual comrades, unschooled workers who don't understand our program, or who misinterpret it—all kinds of provisions are made to try to explain things to them, to convince them of the party's point of view. That is a frequent occurrence, because, after all, the program of the party is a document that represents pretty nearly one hundred years of socialist thought, and we don't expect an unschooled worker who joins the party to understand all those doctrines as precisely as the professional party leaders.

Q: What can you tell us about the differences and degree of knowledge of various members of the party?

A: Well, there is a big difference of various members and of various leaders.

Q: Is it always possible to correct every mistake that every member of the party makes?

MR. SCHWEINHAUT: I object to that.

THE COURT: It seems to me the answer to that is obvious.

MR. SCHWEINHAUT: I will stipulate that it isn't always possible.

MR. GOLDMAN: That is fine.

Q: (By Mr. Goldman): What is the position taken by the party on the question of internationalism?

A: The party is internationalist to the very core.

Q: And what do you mean by that?

A: We believe that the modern world is an economic unit. No country is self-sufficient. It is impossible to solve the accumulated problems of the present day, except on a world scale; no nation is self-sufficient, and no nation can stand alone.

The economy of the world now is all tied together in one unit, and because we think that the solution of the problem of the day—the establishment of socialism—is a world problem, we believe that the advanced workers in every country must collaborate in working toward that goal. We have, from the very beginning of our movement, collaborated with like-minded people in all other countries in trying to promote the socialist movement on a world scale. We have advocated the international organization of the workers, and their cooperation in all respects, and mutual assistance in all respects possible.

Q: Does the party have any attitude on the question of racial or national differences?

A: Yes, the party is opposed to all forms of national chauvinism, race prejudice, discrimination, denigration of races—I mean by that, this hateful theory of the fascists about inferior races. We believe in and we stand for the full equality of all races, nationalities, creeds. It is written in our program that we fight against anti-Semitism and that we demand full and unconditional equality for the Negro in all avenues of life. We are friends of the colonial people, the Chinese, of all those that are victimized and treated as inferiors.

Q: What is the position of the party on socialism as a world system?

A: We not only stand for an international socialist movement, but we believe that the socialist order will be a world order, not a national autarchy which is carried to its absurd extreme by the fascists, who have tried to set up a theory that Germany could be a completely self-sufficient nation in an economic sense, that Italy can be, and so forth. We believe that the wealth of the world, the raw materials of the world, and the natural resources of the world are so distributed over the earth that every country contributes something and lacks something for a rounded and harmonious development of the productive forces of mankind.

We visualize the future society of mankind as a socialist world order which will have a division of labor between the various countries according to their resources, a comradely collaboration between them, and production eventually of the necessities and luxuries of mankind according to a single universal world plan.

Q: Did the party ever belong to an international organization?

A: The party belonged to the Fourth International. It was designated that way to distinguish it from the three other international organizations which had been known in the history of socialism. The first one, the International Working Men's Association was founded under the leadership of Marx in the 1860's and lasted until about 1871.*

The Second International was organized on the initiative of the German, French, and other socialist parties of Europe about 1890, and continues today. It includes those reformist socialist parties and trade unions of Europe, or at least did until they were destroyed by the Hitler scourge.

The Third International was founded under the leadership of Lenin and Trotsky after the Russian Revolution. It was founded in 1919, as a rival of the Second International, the main motive being that the Second International had supported the imperialist war of 1914 and, in the view of the Bolsheviks, had thereby betrayed the interests of the workers.

The Fourth International was organized on the initiative of Trotsky as a rival of the Stalinist Third International. We took part in the initiation of that movement, and we participated in its work up until last December.

Q: And what caused you to cease belonging to it?

A: The passage by Congress of the Voorhis Act, which placed penalties upon organizations that have international affiliation, made that necessary. We called a special convention of the party, and formally severed our relation with the Fourth International in compliance with the Voorhis Act.

Q: What role do Fourth International resolutions play in the party?

A: Well, they have a tremendous moral authority in our party. All the sections of the Fourth International have been autonomous in their national decisions, but the programmatic documents of the Fourth International, wherever they are applicable to American conditions, have a decisive influence with us.

---

* The First International was founded on September 28, 1864, and formally dissolved July 15, 1876.—Ed.

Q: So you accept them, insofar as they are applicable to American conditions?

A: Yes—it is not the letter of the law for us in the sense that our Declaration of Principles is, but it is a general ideological guiding line for us.

Q: Now, does the party interest itself in the trade-union movement?

A: Oh, yes, immensely.

Q: And why?

A: Well, we view the trade-union movement as the basic organization of the workers that should include the great mass of the workers, and must include them, in the struggle to defend their interests from day to day. We are in favor of trade unions, and participate in organizing them wherever we can.

Q: And what is the fundamental purpose of the party in trying to strengthen the trade unions and organizing them wherever they are not organized?

A: Well, we have a double purpose. One is that we are seriously interested in anything that benefits the workers. The trade unions help the workers to resist oppression, possibly to gain improvement of conditions; that is for us a decisive reason to support them, because we are in favor of anything that benefits the workers.

A second reason is that the trade unions, which are big mass organizations, offer the most productive fields for us to work in to popularize the ideas of the party, and the influence of the party.

Q: What instructions, if any, are given to party members with reference to their activity in trade unions?

A: Yes, our party members are instructed to be the best trade unionists, to do the most work for the unions—be most attentive, most active in the union work—to be the best mechanics at their trade, to become influential by virtue of their superiority in their abilities and their actions in behalf of the workers in the union.

Q: Does the party take a position with reference to the CIO and the AFL?

MR. SCHWEINHAUT: I object to that as immaterial, if Your Honor please.

THE COURT: What is the materiality of that, Mr. Goldman?

MR. GOLDMAN: Well, it would explain the fight here in Local 544-CIO, about which the witnesses for the government testified.

THE COURT: He may answer.

THE WITNESS: Yes, we take a position.

Q: (By Mr. Goldman): And what is that position, Mr. Cannon?

A: In general we are in favor of industrial unionism. That is, that form of unionism which organizes all the workers in a given shop or given industry into one union. We consider that a more progressive and effective form of organization than craft unionism, so we support the industrial-union principle.

The CIO has found its greatest field of work in the big mass production industries, such as automobile and steel, which hitherto were unorganized, where the workers were without the protection of any organization, and where experience proved it was impossible for the craft unions, a dozen or more in a single shop, to organize them. We consider that a tremendously progressive development, the organization of several million mass-production workers, so that, in general, we sympathize with the trend represented by the CIO.

But we don't condemn the AFL. We are opposed to craft unionism, but many of our members belong to AFL unions and we have, in general, the same attitude towards them as to CIO unions, to build them up, to strengthen them, improve the conditions of the workers. And we are sponsors of the idea of unity of the AFL and the CIO; it was written in our Declaration of Principles; so that while we are somewhat partial to the CIO as a national movement, we are in favor of unity on the provision that it should not sacrifice the industrial union form of organization.

Q: What is the party policy with reference to the existence of democracy in trade unions?

A: The Declaration of Principles, and all of our editorials and speeches, are continually demanding a democratic regime inside the unions, demanding the rights of the members to speak up, to have free elections, and frequent elections, and in general to have the unions under the control of the rank and file through the system of democracy.

Q: And what is the policy of the party with reference to racketeering and gangsterism in the unions?

A: Similarly, the Declaration of Principles denounces racketeers, gangsters, all criminal elements—summons our members and sympathizers to fight relentlessly to clean them out of the unions, and forbids under penalty of expulsion any member of the party to give any direct or indirect support to any gangster or racketeering element in the unions.

Q: Is there such a policy of the party as controlling the unions?

A: No, a union is an independent, autonomous organization and—

MR. SCHWEINHAUT: Well, now, you have answered the question. He asked you if there was a policy with respect to controlling the unions, and you said, "No."

MR. GOLDMAN: Let him explain.

MR. SCHWEINHAUT: Why does it need explanation?

MR. GOLDMAN: Well, there are at least, I should say, twenty-five or fifty pages of evidence about the party controlling unions.

MR. SCHWEINHAUT: And the witness has said that there is no such policy. That disposes of it.

THE COURT: Well, he has answered this question, certainly.

Q: (By Mr. Goldman): In what way does the party try to win influence in the unions?

A: We try to get our members in the unions to strive for the leading influence in the unions.

Q: How?

A: First of all by our instructions to our members in the unions that they must be the best trade unionists in the union, and they must be the best workers on the job. That is first, in order that they may gain the respect of their fellow workers and their confidence.

Second, they have got to be active in the propagation of our ideas to their fellow workers. They have got to be busy and active in all union affairs—try to get subscriptions to our paper, try to influence union members to come to our lectures and classes and, in general, work to gain sympathy and support for the party and its program. We do say that, surely.

Q: What policy does the party have with reference to placing party members in official positions in the unions?

A: Yes, whenever they can be fairly elected, we certainly encourage them to try.

Q: But through elections?

A: Through elections, yes. Also if they can be appointed by some higher body and the work is not inconsistent with our principles, we advise them to accept the appointment, as in the case, for example, of Comrade Dobbs.

Q: Appointment for what?

A: Dobbs was appointed international organizer of the Teamsters Union at one time.

THE COURT: Ladies and gentlemen of the jury, you will please keep in mind the admonitions of the court. We will recess until ten o'clock tomorrow morning.

District Court of the United States,
District of Minnesota, Fourth Division.

Wednesday, November 19, 1941
Morning Session

James P. Cannon

Direct Examination (continued)

Q: (By Mr. Goldman): Mr. Cannon, will you tell us the position of the Socialist Workers Party on the causes of modern war?

A: Modern wars, in the opinion of our party, are caused by the conflict of imperialist nations for markets, colonies, sources of raw material, fields for investment, and spheres of influence.

Q: What do you mean by "imperialist," Mr. Cannon?

A: Those capitalist nations which directly or indirectly exploit other countries.

Q: What is the party's position on the inevitability of wars under the capitalist system?

A: As long as the capitalist system remains, and with it those conditions which I have mentioned, which flow automatically from the operation of the capitalist and imperialist system, wars, recurring wars, are inevitable.

Q: And can anybody's opposition, including the opposition of the Socialist Workers Party to war, prevent wars under the capitalist system?

A: No. Our party has always stated that it is impossible to prevent wars without abolishing the capitalist system which breeds war. It may be possible to delay a war for a while, but eventually it is impossible to prevent wars while this system, and its conflicts of imperialist nations, remains.

Q: Then is it true that the party is of the opinion that wars are caused by international economic conflicts, and not by the good will or bad will of some people?

A: Yes. That does not eliminate the possibility of incidental attacks being caused by the acts of this or that ruling group of one country or another; but fundamentally wars are caused by the efforts of all the capitalist powers to expand into other fields. The only way they can get them is by taking them away from some other power, because the whole world has been divided up among a small group of imperialist powers. That is what leads to war, regardless of the will of the people.

We do not maintain that the ruling groups of any of the imperialist powers now at war really desired the war. We have stated many times that they would have been glad to have avoided it; but they could not avoid it and maintain the capitalist system in their country.

Q: What is the attitude of the party towards a war which it designates as an imperialist war?

A: Our party is unalterably opposed to all imperialist wars.

Q: And what is meant by opposition to imperialist wars?

A: By that we mean that we do not give any support to any imperialist war. We do not vote for it; we do not vote for any person that promotes it; we do not speak for it; we do not write for it. We are in opposition to it.

Q: How does the Socialist Workers Party oppose the idea of the United States entering into the war?

A: We do it as every other political party promotes its ideas on any foreign policy. We write against it in the paper; we speak against it; we try to create sentiment in any organization we can approach, to adopt resolutions against the war. If we had members in Congress, they would speak in Congress, in the Senate, against it. In general we carry on public political agitation against the entry of the United States into war, and against all measures taken either by the Executive or by Congress which in our opinion lead towards active participation in the war.

Q: What do you mean by "active"?

A: For example, all those measures which have been taken, which put the United States into the war, in effect, without a formal declaration to that effect.

Q: What was the party's position with reference to amending the Constitution to give the people the power to declare war?

A: For quite a while now we have supported the proposal that was introduced into Congress, I think by Representative Ludlow, and is known as the Ludlow Amendment, for an amendment to the Constitution requiring a referendum vote of the people for the declaration of a war. Our party supported this proposal and at times has carried on a very energetic agitation in favor of such an amendment to require a referendum vote of the people before war could be declared.

Q: And that is still the position of the party, Mr. Cannon?

A: Yes, that is incorporated as one of the points of practical daily policy, in the editorial masthead of our paper. If I am not mistaken, it appears on the editorial page as one of our current principles, and every once in a while there appears an editorial or an article in the paper attempting to revive interest in this idea.

Q: If the United States should enter into the European conflict, what form would the opposition of the party take to the war?

A: We would maintain our position.

Q: And that is what?

A: That is, we would not become supporters of the war, even after the war was declared. That is, we would remain an opposition political party on the war question, as on others.

Q: You would not support the war?

A: That is what I mean, we would not support the war, in a political sense.

THE COURT: May I ask you to develop the significance of that last statement?

MR. GOLDMAN: Yes.

Q: When you say, "nonsupport of the war," just exactly what would the party do during a war, which would indicate its nonsupport of the war?

A: Insofar as we are permitted our rights, we would speak against the war as a false policy that should be changed, in the same sense, from our point of view, that other parties might oppose the foreign policy of the government in time of war, just as Lloyd George, for example, opposed the Boer War in public addresses and speeches. Ramsay MacDonald, who later became prime minister of England, opposed the war policy of England during the World War of 1914–1918. We hold our own point of view, which is different from the point of view of the two political figures I have just mentioned, and so far as we are permitted to exercise our right, we would continue to write and speak for a different foreign policy for America.

Q: Would the party take any practical steps, so-called, to show its opposition to war, or nonsupport of the war?

A: Practical steps in what sense?

Q: Would the party try to sabotage the conduct of the war in any way?

A: No. The party has specifically declared against sabotage. We are opposed to sabotage.

Q: What is that—what do you mean by "sabotage"?

A: That is, obstruction of the operation of the industries, of transportation, or the military forces. Our party has never at any time taken a position in favor of obstruction or sabotage of the military forces in time of war.

Q: And will you explain the reasons why?

A: Well, as long as we are a minority, we have no choice but to submit to the decision that has been made. A decision has been made, and is accepted by a majority of the people, to go to war. Our comrades have to comply with that. Insofar as they are eligible for the draft, they must accept that, along with the rest of their generation, and go and perform the duty imposed on them, until such time as they convince the majority for a different policy.

Q: So, essentially, your opposition during a war would be of the same type as your opposition prior to the war?

A: A political opposition. That is what we speak of.

Q: Did the party ever, or does the party now, advise its members or any of its sympathizers, or any workers that it comes in contact with, to create insubordination in the United States armed forces or naval forces?

A: No.

Q: Will you explain the reason why?

A: Fundamentally the reason is the one I just gave. A serious political party, which aims at a social transformation of society, which is possible only by the consent and support of the great mass of the population—such a party cannot attempt while it is a minority to obstruct the carrying out of the decisions of the majority. By sabotage and insubordination, breaking discipline and so on, a party would absolutely discredit itself and destroy its possibilities of convincing people, besides being utterly ineffective so far as accomplishing anything would be concerned.

Q: Will you state the reasons why the party would not support a war conducted by the present government of the United States?

A: In general, we do not put any confidence in the ruling capitalist group in this country. We do not give them any support because we do not think they can or will solve the fundamental social problems which must be solved in order to save civilization from shipwreck.

We believe that the necessary social transition from the present system of capitalism to the far more efficient order of socialism can only be brought about under a leadership of the workers. The workers must organize themselves independently of the capitalist political parties. They must organize a great party of their own, develop an independent working-class party of their own, and oppose the policy of the capitalist parties, regardless of whether they are called the Democratic or Republican, or anything else.

Q: What kind of a war would you consider a war waged by the present government of the United States?

A: I would consider it a capitalist war.

Q: Why?

A: Because America is today a capitalist nation. It is different from the others only in that it is stronger than the others and bigger. We do not believe in capitalist policy. We do not want to gain any colonies. We do not want bloodshed to make profits for American capital.

Q: What is the party's position on the claim that the war against Hitler is a war of democracy against fascism?

A: We say that is a subterfuge, that the conflict between American imperialism and German imperialism is for the domination of the world. It is absolutely true that Hitler wants to dominate the world, but we think it is equally true that the ruling group of American capitalists has the same idea, and we are not in favor of either of them.

We do not think that the Sixty Families who own America want to wage this war for some sacred principle of democracy. We think they are the greatest enemies of democracy here at home. We think they would only use the opportunity of a war to eliminate all civil liberties at home, to get the best imitation of fascism they can possibly get.

Q: What is the position of the party with reference to any imperialist or capitalist enemy of the United States, like Germany or Italy?

A: We are not pro-German. We absolutely are not interested in the success of any of the imperialist enemies of the United States.

Q: In case of a conflict between the United States and Germany, Italy, or Japan, what would the party's position be so far as the victory or defeat of the United States, as against its imperialist enemies?

A: Well, we are certainly not in favor of a victory for Japan or Germany or any other imperialist power over the United States.

Q: Is it true then that the party is as equally opposed to Hitler as it is to the capitalist claims of the United States?

A: That is uncontestable. We consider Hitler and Hitlerism the greatest enemy of mankind. We want to wipe it off the face of the earth. The reason we do not support a declaration of war by American arms is because we do not believe the American capitalists can defeat Hitler and fascism. We think Hitlerism can be destroyed only by way of conducting a war under the leadership of the workers.

Q: What method does the party propose for the defeat of Hitler?

A: If the workers formed the government I spoke of, if the workers' form of government were in power, we would propose two things:

One, that we issue a declaration to the German people, a solemn promise, that we are not going to impose another Versailles peace on them; that we are not going to cripple the German people, or take away their shipping facilities, or take away their milk cows, as was done in the horrible Treaty of Versailles, starving German babies at their mothers' breasts, and filling the German people with such hatred and such demand for revenge that it made it possible for a monster like Hitler to rally them with the slogan of revenge against this terrible Treaty of Versailles. We would say to them:

"We promise you that we will not impose any of those things upon the German people. On the contrary, we propose to you a reorganization of the world on a fair socialist basis, where the

German people, with all their recognized ability and their genius and labor, can participate equally with us." That would be our party's first proposal to them.

Second, we would also say to them, "On the other hand, we are going to build the biggest army and navy and air force in the world, to put at your disposal, to help smash Hitler by force of arms on one front, while you revolt against him on the home front."

I think that would be the program, in essence, of our party, which the workers' and farmers' government of America would advance so far as Hitler is concerned, and we believe that is the only way Hitlerism will be destroyed. Only when the Great Powers on the other side can successfully prevail upon the German people to rise against Hitler, because we must not forget—

MR. SCHWEINHAUT: You have answered the question, Mr. Cannon.

Q: Now, until such time as the workers and farmers in the United States establish their own government and use their own methods to defeat Hitler, the Socialist Workers Party must submit to the majority of the people—is that right?

A: That is all we can do. That is all we propose to do.

Q: And the party's position is that there will be no obstruction of ways and means taken by the government for the effective prosecution of its war?

A: No obstruction in a military way, or by minority revolution; on the contrary, the party has declared positively against any such procedure.

Q: What is the opinion of the party as to the relationship between war and a possible revolutionary situation?

A: Wars frequently have been followed by revolution; wars themselves are the expression of a terrible social crisis, which they are unable to solve. Misery and suffering grow at such a tremendous pace in war, that it often leads to revolution.

The Russo-Japanese war of 1904 produced the Russian revolution of 1905. The World War of 1914 produced the Russian Revolution of 1917, the Hungarian revolution, near-revolution in Italy, and the revolution in Germany and Austria; and in general, a revolutionary situation developed over the whole continent of Europe, as the result of the First World War.

I think it is highly probable that if the war in Europe continues, then the mass of the people, especially in Europe, will undertake to put a stop to the slaughter by revolutionary means.

Q: So that it would be correct to say that a revolutionary situation is created by a war, and not by the Socialist Workers Party, if a revolutionary situation will arise?

A: I would say it is created by the privations of the capitalist system, which are tremendously accelerated by a war.

Q: What is the policy of the party with reference to permitting various opinions and interpretations of current events in the party's publications?

A: Well, it is not prohibited. Usually, individual members of the party write articles with a certain slant on current events that is not necessarily shared by the majority of the Committee.

Q: With reference to predictions or opinions about future occurrences, would you say the party is more liberal in granting that freedom?

A: Yes, it must necessarily be, because predictions are not verifiable, completely, until after the event, and different opinions arise. We have had in the party, especially since the outbreak of the World War, conflicting opinions as to when the United States would make formal entry into the war, or whether or not the United States would enter the war. There were not very many who doubted that it would, but I heard some people in the party express such opinions.

Q: And would you say that the opinions of party members with reference to a possible future revolutionary situation is in that category of opinion, concerning which there are many differences of opinion?

A: Yes, there must necessarily be.

Q: Do you include in that category also predictions as to whether the revolution would not be accompanied by force or not?

A: Well, within limits, within limits. There is more agreement among the educated leaders of the party who have studied history and Marxism—there is more agreement on that question, than on such a question as the prospect of entry into the present World War.

Q: But there can be, and there are, differences of opinion as to the exact time of the revolutionary situation and the approximate development of it?

A: As to the time of a revolution, that is absolutely speculative. There isn't anybody in the party who has anything more than a tentative opinion on that question.

Q: Would you make any distinction between official resolutions of the party and editorials?

A: Yes. A resolution is a formal document, approved by the National Committee itself, or by a convention. It is thought out, and becomes an official statement of the party. In my opinion that carries and should carry a greater weight than an editorial which might be knocked out by an editor while he is rushing the paper to press, and is not written with the same care and preciseness of expression which obtains when a resolution is formally signed by the National Committee.

Q: Does the party accept officially all opinions expressed in signed articles, or even editorials?

A: No, I would say not officially, no. Signed articles by prominent leaders of the party, in the minds of the party members, have at least a semiofficial status, I think, but they do not have the weight of a formal resolution of the Committee or of a convention.

Q: Now will you please explain what is called the military policy of the party?

A: The military policy of the party is incorporated in the decisions of the conference a year ago, in September 1940.

At that time we called a special conference of the party, in connection with a plenary meeting of the National Committee, to consider this particular question, our attitude towards conscription and the further progress of the war situation, and there we adopted a resolution substantially as follows:

Point 1: As long as conscription has been adopted as the law, and once it was the law, referring to the Selective Service Act, all party members must comply with this law, must register and must not oppose the registration of others. On the contrary, the party specifically opposes the position of such groups as conscientious objectors. While we admire the courage and integrity of a rather high order that it takes to do what the conscientious objectors have done, we have written against their policy and said it is wrong for individuals to refuse to register when the great mass of their generation is going to war. So far as we are concerned, if the young generation of American workers goes to war, our party members go with them, and share in all their dangers and hardships and experience.

Point 2: Our resolution says that our comrades have got to be good soldiers, the same way that we tell a comrade in a factory that he must be the best trade unionist and the best mechanic in order to gain the confidence and respect of his fellow workers. We say, in the military service, he must be the best soldier; he must be the most efficient in the use of whatever weapons and arms he is assigned to, and submit to discipline, and be concerned about the welfare of fellow soldiers in order to establish his position in their respect and confidence.

THE COURT: May I inquire whether or not this is an oral or a written policy that Mr. Cannon has just given?

THE WITNESS: I think my speeches at the conference in Chicago last September were introduced as exhibits here, some extracts from them at least.

MR. GOLDMAN: Yes, I am sure they were.

THE COURT: Mr. Myer, you should be able to put your finger on those particular exhibits, I believe.

MR. MYER: I think they are exhibits 116 and 186.

Q: Now, were there any other points discussed and adopted at that conference with reference to the military policy of the party?

A: Yes. We came out in favor of the idea of conscription, universal military training. That is predicated on the idea that at the present time the whole world is in arms, that all decisions nowadays are being made by arms, or with the threat of arms. In such a situation we must recognize that the workers must also become trained in the military arts. We are in favor of universal military training, according to our official decision; but we are not in favor, that is, we do not give political support to the method that is used by the present capitalist government.

We propose that the workers should get military training in special camps under the direction of the trade unions; that the government should furnish a part of its military funds in appropriations to equip those camps with the necessary arms and materials and instructors, but the camps should be under the auspices of the trade unions.

There should be also special camps set up under the auspices of the unions, for the training of workers to become officers. Government funds should be appropriated for this purpose, so that a condition can be created to remove one of the greatest defects and sources of dissatisfaction in the present military apparatus, that is, the social gulf between the worker or farmer-soldier, and the officer from another class, who does not have an understanding of the soldier's problem and does not have the proper attitude towards him.

We believe the workers are entitled to have as officers men out of their own ranks whom they have learned to respect in the course of their work and common struggle with them, such as picket captains, leaders of unions, men who have distinguished themselves in the affairs of workers' organizations, and who come from the rank and file of the workers. Such men as officers would be much more concerned about the welfare of the rank and file of soldiers than a college boy from Harvard or Yale, who never saw a factory, and never rubbed elbows with the worker, and considers him an inferior being. That is, I would say, the heart of our military proposal, of our military policy.

Q: What is the position of the party with reference to civil rights in the army?

A: We stand also for soldier citizens' rights. We do not agree with the idea that when you take a million and a half young men out of civil life, that they cease to have the rights of citizens. We think they should have all the rights of citizens. They should have the right to petition Congress; they should have the right to vote; they should have the right to elect committees to present their grievances; they should have the right to elect their own officers, at least the minor officers; and in general they should have the democratic rights of citizens, and we advocate that. We advocate legislation to confer upon the soldiers those rights, and doing away with the present inefficient military setup.

Q: Did the party officially, or to your knowledge, did any party member now in the service, ever attempt to create insubordination in the ranks of the armed forces?

A: Not to my knowledge.

Q: In your opinion, if there have been such incidents, what is the cause of them?

A: I think there are a number of causes of discontent and dissatisfaction in the conscript army. That is a matter of public comment in all the newspapers and magazines, and various opinions and theories have been expressed as to the reasons for it.

Q: How does the party propose to realize the demands for compulsory training under trade-union control?

A: Our program is a legislative program. Everything that we propose we would have incorporated into law. If we had a delegation in Congress, they would introduce a bill, or a series of bills, providing for the incorporation in the law of the country of these proposals, these military proposals of ours.

Q: Did any authoritative leader of the party ever refer to Plattsburg as an example?

A: Yes. In fact, that was part of the origin of the idea. As I said before, the chief sore point in the military setup is the class distinction between the officers and the ranks. We know that in the period prior to the First World War, special camps were set up for the training of business and professional men to be officers in the army. Plattsburg was one of these. This was a part of the so-called preparedness campaign, before the United States finally got into the war. The government appropriated some funds, and some businessmen donated funds. The government provided instructors and furnished the necessary equipment for the training of a large number of business and professional men who were ultimately to be officers in the army.

We cannot see why the workers should not have the same rights. We think it is perfectly fair and reasonable, certainly it is compatible with the existing laws. As I said before, it is a legislative proposal on our part. We would, if we could, incorporate that into the law of the country.

THE COURT: We will take our morning recess at this time.

(Morning Recess)

Q: I call your attention, Mr. Cannon, to the testimony of some witnesses for the prosecution to the effect that certain party members told them to join the army, and then to start to kick about the food and create dissatisfaction. What can you say with reference to the party policy about that?

A: In the military forces, as far as our information goes from members who have been drafted and from others whom—

MR. SCHWEINHAUT: Now, just a moment. You are not answering the question at all. He asked you whether the party had a policy, whether it does or does not. If so, tell us what that policy is, not what you heard from people in the service.

THE WITNESS: I want to explain why our policy is what it is.

THE COURT: We have not heard that there is a policy yet.

Q: Is there a policy?

A: Yes, we have a policy.

Q: What is that policy?

A: The policy is not to support or to initiate any agitation about food. I want to tell you the reason. So far as our knowledge goes, from members of the party who have been drafted and whom we have seen on furlough, and from other investigation, there is not much dissatisfaction with the food in the present setup.

Q: And if there is any dissatisfaction with food, what would you say it was caused by?

A: So far as our information goes, there are only isolated cases now. We do not propose to kick about the food if the food is satisfactory. If the food is bad, the soldiers will kick about it themselves, and they should kick about it.

Q: What would you say about the testimony of these witnesses—

MR. SCHWEINHAUT: I object to that.

MR. GOLDMAN: Strike it out.

Q: Then will you state definitely, what is the policy of the party with reference to creating dissatisfaction in the army when causes for dissatisfaction do not exist?

A: I do not know of anything in the party program or party literature that proposes to incite grievances without foundation. Where causes for dissatisfaction exist, they create the dissatisfaction, not the party.

MR. SCHWEINHAUT: Just a moment, please.

Q: If there have been grievances, and if there has been dissatisfaction, is the party in any way responsible for that?

A: No, I don't think so, in any way at all. That is the present situation.

Q: And the people who have charge of feeding the army are the ones responsible for that, or for the grievances?

MR. SCHWEINHAUT: Well, that is leading.

MR. GOLDMAN: Well, he has not objected, so you may proceed and answer it.

MR. SCHWEINHAUT: Then I will object to it now.

THE COURT: I will sustain the objection.

Q: Now, on the question of military training under trade union control—you were speaking about Plattsburg at the time of the recess. Will you continue and explain further the policy on that?

A: I used that as an illustration of how special camps were instituted and government instructors provided to train business and professional men in the period shortly prior to our entry into the last World War. In the Spanish Civil War all the parties and unions not only had their own training camps authorized by the government, but even supplied their own regiments in the fight against the fascist army of Franco.

Q: Now, the present trade unions are not under the control of the party, are they?

A: No, they are under the control, essentially or practically completely, of leaders who are in harmony with the present Roosevelt administration.

Q: As I understand, the party favors military training under trade-union control?

A: Yes. The idea is to give to the unions, as they are, a wider authority and supervision over their people.

Q: And that policy is not dependent upon the party controlling the trade unions?

A: No. We can only take our chances that we will be in the minority in those training camps, as we are in the unions.

Q: What measures do you propose in order to effectuate the policy of military training under trade-union control?

A: As I think I said before, it is a proposal for a legislative program. We would have such a bill introduced into Congress and passed, if we had the power, or if we could gain the support of congressmen who are opposed to us on other grounds, but who would agree to this. This is a program that is not necessarily socialist.

Q: If any member of the party would either attempt to obstruct the Selective Service Act, or advise the obstruction of it, what would the party do about that?

MR. SCHWEINHAUT: That is objected to on the ground that there has been no evidence offered by the government that the party attempted to obstruct the Selective Service Act.

MR. GOLDMAN: Then the government admits that the party has not attempted to obstruct the Selective Service Act?

MR. SCHWEINHAUT: We have not attempted to show that there was any attempt to interfere with the Selective Service Act.

MR. GOLDMAN: I gathered that questions were asked a number of witnesses, as to their age, and the necessity of their going into service, with an intention on the part of the prosecution to prove that we, somehow or other, tried to interfere. If the government says "No," I will drop that.

MR. SCHWEINHAUT: We will clear the atmosphere on that right now. We do not contend that the party attempted to keep anybody from registering for the draft, or in that respect to impede the progress of the Selective Service Act. What our evidence tended to show was what the party members were supposed to do after they got into the army.

MR. GOLDMAN: Well, that is cleared up then.

Q: Did you hear a witness for the government testify that he was told by some party member to go to Fort Snelling and create dissatisfaction? I think that was the gist of the testimony. Did you hear that?

A: Something to that effect.

Q: What is the party's policy with reference to any creating of dissatisfaction in Fort Snelling or any other military camp?

MR. SCHWEINHAUT: I object to that, because he has answered what it was at least twice.

THE COURT: Objection sustained.

Q: Does the party have an official position on the Russian Revolution, Mr. Cannon?

A: Yes.

Q: What is that position? Has it ever been adopted in the form of an official resolution?

A: It is incorporated in the Declaration of Principles.

Q: What is that position?

A: That the party supports—

MR. SCHWEINHAUT: Just a moment. I will object to that on the ground that, the witness having stated that it is incorporated in the Declaration of Principles, therefore, it speaks for itself.

MR. GOLDMAN: An explanation of the Declaration of Principles is in order.

THE COURT: He may answer.

A: (Continuing): We support the Russian Revolution of 1917. We consider that it embodies the doctrines and the theories of Marxism which we uphold.

Q: How many revolutions were there in Russia in 1917?

A: There was a revolution in February according to the Russian calendar, in March according to the modern calendar, which developed into the proletarian revolution of November 7 according to the modern calendar.

Q: What is the general position taken by Marxists with reference to the Russian Revolution?

A: The one that I have given here, in support of the revolution.

Q: And what does "support" mean?

A: Well, that is a rather mild—it would be a mild description of our attitude. We consider it the greatest and most progressive event in the entire history of mankind.

Q: And I think you said in your reply to a previous question, that you consider the doctrines embodied in that revolution as Marxist doctrines? Explain that.

A: The theory of Marxism in our opinion was completely vindicated in the Russian Revolution, and the theory of Marxism, which is the establishment of a government of workers and peasants, which undertakes to bring about a social transformation from capitalism towards socialism—all this was undertaken in the Russian Revolution.

Q: Now, can you tell us anything about the legality of that revolution?

A: Yes.

THE COURT: Judged by what standards?

MR. GOLDMAN: What I mean by that is to have him explain exactly how the revolution occurred, because counsel for the government tries to present it as a violent upheaval of the minority against the majority, and the facts are the very contrary. I want the witness to explain the nature of that revolution.

A: The czar and czarism were overthrown in March by an uprising of the masses, of the people in the big cities, and the peasants.

Q: Was the Bolshevik Party responsible for that uprising in any way?

A: No. The Bolshevik Party was a very infinitesimal group at the time of the March revolution.

Q: What is the meaning of "Bolshevism"?

A: The world *Bolshevik* is a Russian word meaning *majority*. It acquired a political meaning in the Russian Social Democratic Labor Party. In the Congress of 1903 a controversy developed which divided the party into groups, the majority and the minority, the majority called the Bolsheviks and the minority called Mensheviks.

Q: Those are Russian words meaning minority and majority?

A: Yes. They split up and divided into parties. Each called itself the Russian Social-Democratic Labor Party and in parentheses on the end "Bolsheviks" or "Mensheviks," as the case might be.

Q: Now, will you proceed and tell the jury what happened during the October Revolution, or in our calendar in November 1917.

A: Well, to show the chronology: When czarism was overthrown by the masses of the people, the whole structure of that tyranny was destroyed. A new government was constituted, but the new government machinery was based on the Soviets, which sprang up spontaneously in the revolutionary upheaval. Soviets of workers and soldiers were established everywhere. In Petrograd, the workers and soldiers sent delegates—deputies—to the central council or, as they called it, the Soviet; similarly in Moscow and other places. This body was recognized as authoritative.

The government that was constituted after the overthrow of the czar was headed by Prince Lvov, with Miliukov as foreign minister; it derived its authority from the Soviets of Workers' and Soldiers' Deputies and the Soviets of Peasants' Deputies. In April they had a National All-Russian Conference of the Workers' and Soldiers' Soviets, and there they elected an All-Russian Central Executive Committee of the Workers' and Soldiers' Soviets. In May, the peasant Soviets had an All-Russian Congress and elected an All-Russian Central Executive Committee of the peasants.

Q: What proportion of the population did those Soviets represent?

A: They represented the people, the great mass of the people. I think it was impossible even to speak in terms of majorities or minorities. They were the masses themselves. The peasants and the soldiers and the workers were the people; those two bodies, the All-Russian Central Executive Committee of the Workers' and Soldiers' Soviets and the All-Russian Central Executive Committee of the Peasant Soviets, formed a joint body which was recognized as the most authoritative and representative body in Russia. It was by their consent that the government cabinet ruled.

The All-Russian Executive Committee of the Soviets repudiated Miliukov, who was the leader of the bourgeoisie. The Soviet body opposed him because of his foreign policy, involving secret treaties that had been exposed. He therefore had to resign, because without the support of the Soviets, authority was lacking; and I think that could be likened, as an analogy, to the French system of the resignation of the prime minister when there is a no-confidence vote in the Chamber.

Q: So that the Soviets constituted the authority of the people of Russia?

A: That is right.

Q: In what way did the Bolsheviks progress to power?

A: I wish to go on with the chronology, if you will permit me. Following the fall of Miliukov, Kerensky rose—there is a popular impression in this country that he became premier with the fall of the czar. That is not so. Kerensky became premier in July. He was made a minister and eventually premier because he was a member of the Social Revolutionary Party. That was the peasant party, which then lead the Soviets. He was also supported by the worker element, because he had been a labor lawyer. That was the basis of Kerensky's office; that is, his authority was derived directly from the Soviets.

Now in this period the Bolsheviks were a small minority. They did not create the Soviets. The Soviets were created by the masses; they were initiated by the masses. Neither the Bolshevik Party nor any other party could do anything without the support of the Soviets. In the midst of the revolution of 1905 and again in the overthrow of the czar in 1917, the Soviets sprang up simultaneously.

The most influential one naturally was in Petrograd, which was the seat of government. The Bolsheviks were a small minority in this Soviet at the time of the overthrow of the czar. When Kerensky became premier, the combination of his Social Revolutionary Party and the Menshevik Socialist Party—those two parties together had an overwhelming majority in the Soviets, and ruled by virtue of that. The Bolsheviks were an opposing faction.

During that time Lenin, as the spokesman for the Bolsheviks, said over and over again, "As long as we are in the minority in the Soviets, all we can do is patiently explain." The Bolshevik Party opposed any attempt to seize power by a putsch.

Q: What is a "putsch"?

A: An armed action of a small group. The Bolshevik Party demanded, with Lenin as their spokesman, that the Social Revolutionary Party and the Menshevik Party take complete control of the government by removing the bourgeois ministers and make it a completely labor and peasant government, and they issued the promise that, "If you do that, we promise that as long as we are in the minority, we will not try to overthrow you. We will not support you politically, we will criticize you, but we will not undertake to overthrow the government as long as we are in the minority." That was the policy of the Bolsheviks in the March days of the revolution against the czar, and into July.

In July the workers in Petrograd staged a demonstration with arms, against the advice of the Bolsheviks. The Bolsheviks advised against it on the ground that it might unduly provoke the situation, and tried to persuade the workers in Petrograd not to go into that action. It was not a rebellion; it was simply a parade with arms. This action, carried out by the Petrograd workers against the advice of the Bolsheviks, brought repressions against the workers on the part of the Kerensky government.

Then the Kerensky government undertook to discredit and frame up the Bolshevik Party. They accused Lenin and Trotsky of being German spies. This was the predecessor of Stalin's Moscow trials. They accused Lenin and Trotsky and the Bolsheviks of being German spies. Trotsky was thrown into jail,

Lenin was forced into hiding, and repressions continued against the Bolsheviks, but it did not do any good, because the policy and slogans of the Bolsheviks were growing in popularity. One by one the great factories and soldiers' regiments began to vote in favor of the Bolshevik program.

In September an attempt at counterrevolution was made under the leadership of General Kornilov, who could be properly described as a Russian monarchist-fascist. He organized an army and undertook to overthrow the Kerensky government in Petrograd, with the idea of restoring the old regime.

The Kerensky government, that had put Trotsky in jail, had to release him from prison to get the support of his party to fight down the counterrevolutionary army of Kornilov.

Trotsky was brought from prison and went directly to the Military Revolutionary Committee, in which government men also sat, and there drew up with them plans for a joint fight against Kornilov. Kornilov was crushed; the counterrevolution was crushed primarily by the workers under the inspiration of the Bolshevik Party. They tied up his railroad trains; he could not move his troops; his best troops were induced to fight against him, and his counterrevolution was crushed.

As this was going on, the Bolsheviks became more popular all the time, as the genuine representatives of the revolution. They gained the majority in the Petrograd Soviet, the most influential Soviet in the country, and in Moscow and others. The Kerensky government was losing ground because it was not solving any of the problems of the people. The Bolsheviks' slogans of "Bread," "Peace," "Land," and other slogans—those were the slogans that the masses wanted.

On November 7 was held the Congress of the All-Russian Soviets of Workers and Soldiers. The Bolsheviks had a majority there, and simultaneously with the meeting of the Soviets, where the Bolsheviks had a majority, they took the governmental power.

Q: And was there any violence connected with the gaining of the majority by the Bolsheviks?

A: Very little—just a little scuffling, that's all.

MR. SCHWEINHAUT: That was in Petrograd?

THE WITNESS: In Petrograd, yes. That was also where the czar was overthrown.

Q: And subsequent to the gaining of the majority by the Bolsheviks what violence, if any, occurred?

A: One point more first. A month or so later, a special All-Russian Congress of the Peasant Soviets met, and there also the Bolsheviks had a majority. Then the minority withdrew from those authoritative bodies of government, and began an opposition struggle against the Bolshevik government.

Q: What violence, if any, occurred, and who initiated the violence?

A: That began following the armed struggle against the government.

Q: Who began it?

A: The czarists, the white guard Russian element, the bourgeoisie generally, the deposed capitalists and others. They undertook a counterrevolution, and the civil war that ensued lasted until almost 1921. The civil war lasted so long because the white guard and bourgeois elements received the support, first of the Germans, and then of England and France, and even the United States sent an expedition.

The Soviet government had to fight against the whole capitalist world, on top of fighting against their own opposition at home; and the fact that the Bolsheviks represented the great majority of the people was best evidenced by the fact that they were victorious in this civil war, not only against their opponents at home, but also against the outside powers who supplied the opposition with arms, soldiers and funds.

Q: How were the Soviets in those days elected?

A: They were elected in the factory-workers' meetings; that is, the factory workers would gather to elect their delegate. Each Soviet constituted a unit of government, and the combination of Soviets constituted the government.

In the Soviet system, the factories select delegates, according to their number, one for each thousand or whatever the proportion may be. The soldiers' regiments do the same; the peasants or dirt farmers do the same, so that the government established in that way, by those Soviets, represents the whole mass of the people who are involved in productive activity.

Q: What was the number of members of the Bolshevik Party at the time of the Russian Revolution in November 1917?

A: The most authoritative figure I have seen given is 260,000, or a quarter of a million. That seems to be the figure that has the best authority.

A: And what proportion of the population supported the Bolshevik Party at that time?

A: In my opinion, the great majority of the workers, peasants and soldiers supported them at the time they took power and afterwards.

Q: From which group or class of society did the Bolshevik Party get most of its members?

A: From the workers. It was a workers' party, a party of industrial workers and agricultural laborers. There were some peasants in the party, but the party was primarily constituted of industrial workers in the cities, agricultural laborers, and some intellectuals, some educated people who had put themselves at the service of the workers in the party.

Q: What is the best authority as to the number of workers in Russia at the time of the revolution—by "workers" meaning industrial workers?

A: Five million.

Q: And the majority of the population consisted of peasants?

A: Peasants, yes.

Q: What is your opinion as to the number of members that the Socialist Workers Party will probably have when the majority of people in this country adopt the program of the party?

MR. SCHWEINHAUT: I object to that, Your Honor.

THE COURT: What is the basis of your objection?

MR. SCHWEINHAUT: He is asking this witness to guess today as to the number of members that the Socialist Workers Party will have when a majority of the people in the United States adopt its policy.

THE COURT: There are too many elements of speculation in that. Objection sustained.

Q: Will you tell the court and jury what differences arose between Stalin and Trotsky subsequent to the revolution?

MR. SCHWEINHAUT: I object to that, because I do not see any materiality or relevancy in it.

MR. GOLDMAN: The prosecution has contended, and I think Mr. Anderson has made many statements to the effect, that Trotsky, being the archconspirator in this case, had certain ideas and certain doctrines. I think the jury is entitled to know in a general way—it is impossible to go into great detail—but the government has opened up its case in such a way that it is essential for the jury to know at least some of the basic principles of Trotsky, who it is alleged was one of the archconspirators.

THE COURT: Well, if you will agree to limit it to a reasonable amount of testimony.

MR. GOLDMAN: I certainly will—otherwise, we might be here two years.

Mr. Anderson: All we ever brought out, on Trotsky, was some literature and speeches and pamphlets, in the party press.

MR. GOLDMAN: I should think that after the prosecution takes three weeks, that they should give me a week at least to try the case.

THE COURT: I don't think it is necessary to try it that way.

Q: Will you describe briefly the fundamental differences that arose between Stalin and Trotsky subsequent to the revolution?

A: I mentioned the other day that the fight originated in the struggle over democracy. That was the origin of the fight, really inspired by Lenin during his last illness, in collaboration with Trotsky. Lenin did not survive to take part in the fight, and Trotsky had to lead it. This soon developed further.

It soon became apparent to critical observers, this tendency of Stalin to crush democracy in the party and in the life of the country generally. It was based on Stalin's desire to change the program and the course of direction of the revolution, which could only be done by this means. Trotsky struggled for free discussion of the problem, with the confidence that the majority of the workers in the party would support his program. Stalin and his group represented, in our opinion, the conservative tendency, based upon a certain stratum of the party and the government that had acquired official positions and privileges and wanted to stop there.

Q: Stalin then represented in your opinion the party of the bureaucratic?

A: The bureaucratic and conservative. As a matter of fact, Trotsky designated it as the bureaucratic-conservative faction, at one stage in the struggle.

Q: Interested in what?

A: It was interested in preserving its privileges, and not extending and developing the benefits for the great mass of the people.

Q: What form did this dictatorship of Stalin assume?

A: It assumed the form of crushing democracy inside of the Communist Party and establishing a dictatorial regime there. For example—

MR. SCHWEINHAUT: Well, while Mr. Cannon is pausing, may I object now to this line of testimony because it is immaterial and irrelevant to the issues here? It is immaterial what form of government Stalin set up in Russia. What do we care?

THE COURT: I do not see any reason why he should go into all the details. I think you should recognize that, Mr. Goldman. I want to give you every opportunity, every reasonable opportunity, to present your theory of the case before the jury, but I do think that there is much here that is immaterial and unnecessary.

Q: What is the position of the party on the Soviet Union at present?

MR. SCHWEINHAUT: I object to that, Your Honor.

THE COURT: He may answer that.

A: The characterization we make of the Soviet Union, as it is today, is of a workers' state, created by the revolution of November 1917, distorted by the bad present regime, and even degenerated, but nevertheless retaining its basic character as a workers' state, because it is based on nationalized industry and not on private property.

Q: Now, what is the position of the party towards the defense of the Soviet Union, and why?

A: We are in favor of defending the Soviet Union against

imperialist powers for the reason I just gave, because we consider it a progressive development, as a workers' state, that has nationalized industry and has eliminated private capitalism and landlordism. That is the reason we defend it.

Q: That is, you consider the Russian or the Soviet state, a state based on the expropriation of private industry from the capitalists?

A: Yes, the operation of industry as a nationalized industry.

Q: And you are defending that kind of a state?

A: Yes.

Q: Isn't it a fact that Stalin has killed most all of the so-called Trotskyists in Russia?

A: Yes. We are against Stalin, but not against the Soviet form of industrial production.

THE COURT: The jury will keep in mind the admonition heretofore given them, and we will now recess until two o'clock this afternoon.

District Court of the United States,
District of Minnesota, Fourth Division.

Wednesday, November 19, 1941
Afternoon Session

THE COURT: Proceed, gentlemen.

James P. Cannon

resumed the stand, having been previously duly sworn,
and testified further as follows:

Direct Examination (continued) by Mr. Goldman:

Q: And the party would exhaust all the possibilities for a peaceful transformation if the democratic rights are given to the working masses?

A: In my opinion, to the very end, yes.

Q: Even to the end of trying to amend the Constitution of the United States, as provided for by the Constitution of the United States?

A: If the democratic processes are maintained here, if they are not disrupted by the introduction of fascist methods by the government, and the majority of the people supporting the ideas of socialism can secure a victory by the democratic processes, I don't see any reason why they cannot proceed, continue to proceed, by the democratic method of amending the Constitution to fit the new regime.

Naturally, the amendments would have to be of a very drastic character, but parts of the Constitution I would be willing to write into the program of the party at any time—that is the Bill of Rights, which we believe in. That section of the Constitution which protects private property rights, we think, would absolutely have to be changed in the society which we envisage, which eliminates private property in industrial enterprises of a large-scale nature.

Q: But it is your belief, is it not, that in all probability the minority will not allow such a peaceful transformation?

A: That is our opinion. That is based on all the historical precedents of the unwillingness of any privileged class, no matter how it is outlived, to leave the scene without trying to impose its will on the majority by force. I cited examples yesterday.

Q: What is the—

A: I might give you another example on the same point. For example, the Bolshevik revolution in Hungary was accomplished without the shedding of one drop of blood, in a completely peaceful manner.

Q: When was that?

A: That was in 1919. The government that was established following the war, of which Count Karolyi was premier, came to what is considered the end of its resources—it could not control the country, did not have the support of the masses, and Count Karolyi as head of the government, on his own motion, went to the head of the Bolshevik Party, or the Communist Party, rather, of Hungary, who was in prison, and summoned him to take charge of the government in a peaceful, legal manner, like the change of a cabinet in the French Parliament—of course, prior to the Petain regime.

Then this Soviet government, having been established in this way, peacefully, was confronted by an uprising of the privileged class, of the landlords and the big owners, who organized an armed fight against the government and eventually overthrew it. The violence on a mass scale followed the change of the government, did not precede it.

Q: What is the position that the party gives to Karl Marx and his doctrines?

A: Karl Marx was the originator of the theories and doctrines and social analyses, which we know as scientific socialism, or Marxism, upon which the entire movement of scientific socialism has been based since his day.

In the *Communist Manifesto* of 1848 his ideas were sketched and then in other big volumes, notably in *Capital,* he made a most exhaustive scientific analysis of the laws governing the operation of capitalist society, showed how the contradictions within it would lead to its downfall as a social system, showed how the conflict of interests between the employers and the workers would represent an uninterrupted class struggle until the workers gained the upper hand and instituted the society of socialism.

So Karl Marx can be viewed not only as the founder of our movement, but as the most authoritative representative of its ideology.

Q: Does the party accept all of the statements found in all of the books written by Karl Marx?

A: No, the party has never obligated itself to do that. We do not consider even Marx as infallible. The party accepts his basic ideas and theories as its own basic ideas and theories. That does not prohibit the party or members of the party from disagreeing with things said or written by Marx which do not strike at the fundamental basis of the movement, of the doctrine.

Q: And you interpret Marx, or you apply the Marxian theories, under conditions that prevail at the present time, is that right?

A: Yes. You see, we don't understand Marxian theory as a

revelation, as a dogma. Engels expressed it by saying our theory is not a dogma but a guide to action, which means that it is a method which the students of Marxism must understand and learn how to apply. One can read every letter and every line written by Marx and still not be a useful Marxist, if one does not know how to apply it to the conditions of his own time. There have been such people, whom we call pedants. *Paying too much attention to smalls details and rules*

Q: You are acquainted with the *Communist Manifesto,* are you not? *Conocedor*

A: Yes.

Q: And you remember—I think it is the last clause of the *Manifesto,* where Marx and Engels, co-authors, say: "We disdain to conceal our aims," and mention something to the effect about violent revolution. Do you remember that?

A: Well, it says, "We disdain to conceal our aims. We openly say that they can be achieved only by the forcible overthrow of all existing social institutions."

Q: When was the *Communist Manifesto* written?

A: 1848.

Q: Subsequent to the writing of the *Communist Manifesto,* did Marx ever write anything with reference to the possibility of a peaceful revolution in democratic countries?

A: Yes.

Q: Where was that written, and explain to the jury what was said.

A: Well, the most authoritative place where it is stated and explained is in the introduction to the first volume of Marx's masterwork, called *Capital,* the introduction by Frederick Engels, who was his co-worker, who was the co-author of the *Communist Manifesto,* and is recognized universally in the movement as completely identified with all of Marx's ideas and theories. Engels as a matter of fact edited and compiled the second two volumes of *Capital,* after the death of Marx.

Q: What did he say in that introduction?

A: This was the English translation of *Capital* and the introduction was presenting the volume to the English public.

Engels stated—I think I can quote almost literally—that he thinks the work of a man who during his entire life was of the opinion that the social transformation in England, at least, could be effected by purely peaceful and legal means—he thought such a book should have a hearing from the English public. That is very close to a literal report of what he stated in this introduction.

Q: And why did Marx have that opinion with reference to England?

A: Well, he had that opinion with reference to England as distinct from the autocratic countries, because of its parliamentary system, its democratic processes, and civil libertarian method of political procedure.

Q: So at the time that Marx and Engels wrote the *Communist Manifesto* in 1848, there was no democracy in existence on the European continent, is that right?

A: The whole of Europe was seething with revolutions at that time.

Q: And no democratic processes were available?

A: At least not in the stable system that had been established in England. I think I should add, to get the whole picture of this introduction which I am speaking of, that Engels said, after he had made this remark which I have reported, he said: "To be sure, Marx did not exclude the possibility of a proslavery rebellion on the part of the outmoded and dispossessed ruling class." That is, after the transfer of power.

THE COURT: Pardon me, Mr. Cannon. Would you be good enough to elaborate a bit upon the significance of that proslavery phrase?

THE WITNESS: Yes. I think he had in mind the American Civil War. Marx and Engels attentively followed the American Civil War, wrote extensively about it in the *New York Tribune*. A collection of those writings, both political and military, has been published as a book, which is a classic in our movement. And what Marx undoubtedly had in mind when he spoke of a "proslavery rebellion," was an analogy with the American Civil War, which he had characterized as a proslavery rebellion on the part of the Southern slave owners. Of course, he did not maintain that the English bourgeoisie are slave holders in the same sense, but that they exploit the workers.

Q: Now what, in your opinion, is the relationship between the Declaration of Principles of the Socialist Workers Party and the theories of Karl Marx?

A: I would say that insofar as we understand Marxism and are able to apply it, it is an application of the Marxian theories and doctrines, his whole system of ideas, to the social problem in America.

Q: That is, the Declaration of Principles is based then upon the fundamental theories of Karl Marx?

A: Yes, we consider it a Marxist document.

Q: What is the position that the party gives to Lenin?

A: Lenin, in our judgment, was the greatest practical leader of the labor movement and the Russian Revolution, but not on the plane of Marx in the theoretical field. Lenin was a disciple of Marx, not an innovator in theory. To be sure he contributed very important ideas, but to the end of his life he based himself on Marx, as a disciple in the Marxist movement of the world. He holds a position of esteem on a level with Marx, with this distinction between the merits of the two.

Q: Does the party, or do party members agree with every-thing that Lenin ever wrote and published?

A: No. The same attitude applies to Lenin as to Marx. That is, the basic ideas and doctrines practiced, promulgated, and carried out by Lenin, are supported by our movement, which does not exclude the possibility of differing with him about this or that particular writing, or of individual members of the party differing with Lenin in important respects, as has been the case more than once in our party.

Q: By the way, is it true that there is a communist govern-ment in the Soviet Union?

A: No, not in our view.

Q: Is it true that there is communism in the Soviet Union?

A: No there isn't any communism in the Soviet Union.

Q: Is there socialism in the Soviet Union?

A: No—well, I would like to clarify that now. Socialism and communism are more or less interchangeable terms in the Marxist movement. Some make a distinction between them in this respect; for example, Lenin used the expression socialism as the first stage of communism, but I haven't found any other authority for that use. I think that is Lenin's own particular idea. I, for example, consider the terms socialism and communism interchangeable, and they relate to the classless society based on planned production for use as distinct from a system of capitalism based on private property and production for profit.

Q: Could there be a socialist society and a dictatorship like Stalin has at the present time?

a provector

A: No. According to Marx and Engels, as you approach the classless socialist or communist society, the government, instead of becoming more of a factor in human affairs, becomes less and less and eventually withers away and disappears, and is replaced or evolves into an administrative body that does not employ repression against the people.

So the very term government implies, in our terminology, a class society—that is, a class that is dominant and a class that is being suppressed. That holds true whether it is a capitalist government, which in our views oppresses or suppresses the workers and the farmers and represents the interests of the big capital, or a workers' and farmers' government immediately following a revolution which represents the interests of the workers and farmers and suppresses any attempt of the displaced capitalist class to resist its authority or to reestablish its rule.

But once the resistance of the old outlived exploiting class is broken and its members become reconciled to the new society and become assimilated in it, find their place in it, and the struggle between classes which is the dominating factor in all class societies is done away with, because of the disappearance of class distinctions, then the primary function of government as a repressive instrument disappears and the government withers away with it. This is the profound conception of

Marx and Engels that is adhered to by all their disciples.

Q: Did Lenin ever use the term "Blanquism" to designate a certain type of movement?

THE COURT: What is that?

MR. GOLDMAN: Blanquism.

THE WITNESS: Yes, he wrote more than one article in the course of the Russian Revolution, more than once he wrote, "We are not Blanquists."

Q: Now, what is meant by "Blanquism"?

A: Blanqui was a figure in the French revolutionary movement who had followers in the Paris Commune of 1871. Blanqui had his own conception of party and of revolution, and his ideas are known among the students of the history of the labor movement as Blanquism.

Q: What are his ideas?

A: Blanqui's idea was that a small group of determined men, tightly disciplined, could effect the revolution with a coup d'etat.

Q: What is a "coup d'etat"?

A: That is a seizure of power, a seizure of state power by armed action of a small, determined, disciplined group; they would, so to speak, make the revolution for the masses.

Q: And what did Lenin say about that?

A: Lenin opposed this view and his articles were written in answer to opponents who had accused the Bolsheviks of aiming to seize power without a majority. He said, "We are not Blanquists. We base ourselves on mass parties and mass movements, and as long as we are in the minority our task is to patiently explain the problems and issues until we gain the majority, and as long as we are in the minority we will not try to overthrow you. You let us have our freedom of speech and press, give us the opportunity to expound our ideas, and you don't need to fear any Blanquist putsch on our part." Putsch, as I explained before, is an attempt of a small group to seize power by surprise tactics.

Q: So Lenin depended upon mass parties and upon gaining a majority for those mass parties, did he?

A: Yes, in the early days of the Communist International—it is a period that I am familiar with through close study and personal participation in the movement—he hammered at this idea all the time, not only against his critics in Russia, but against various individuals and groups who came toward support of the Russian Revolution, and had some distorted ideas.

In Germany, for example in March 1921, the German party, which had been organized, attempted an insurrection without having the support of the masses; this became famous in the literature of our international movement, as "the March Action." The tactics embodied in it, the conception of some of the German leaders that they could force the revolution by their own determination and sacrifices—this whole idea, the March Action, and all the ideas embodied in it, were condemned by the Third Congress of the Communist International at the insistence of Lenin and Trotsky. They refuted this theory, and they counterposed to it mass parties, mass movements, gaining the majority.

They put out the slogan to the German party that it should aim to have a million members. Zinoviev, who was chairman of the Comintern, made that one of his leading ideas on the German question, that the task of the German party was not to get impatient or to try to force history but to be busy with agitation and propaganda and have the goal of a million in the party.

Q: These million members would not by themselves make any revolution, would they?

A: Naturally not—Lenin did not expect to have a majority of the population become members of the party, but to support the party. But the very fact that he proposed—or rather, Zinoviev, who was the lieutenant of Lenin, acting as chairman of the Communist International proposed—as a slogan, "A million members in the German Party," certainly was a powerful indication that they did not expect to get a majority of the people until they had a numerically powerful party.

Q: Now, what relationship, if any, did Leon Trotsky have to the Socialist Workers Party?

A: Our movement in 1928—when our faction was expelled from the Communist Party—we had adopted the program of Trotsky.

We supported his program from the very beginning—and this was long before we had any personal contact with him. He had been expelled from the Russian party and was exiled in the Asiatic wilderness at a place called Alma Ata. We had no communication with him. We did not know where he was, whether he was dead or alive, but we had one of his important programmatic documents which was called *The Criticism of the Draft Program of the Comintern*. This book elaborated his theories as against those of Stalin at great length and in fundamental respects. This was adopted by us as our own program and from the very beginning we proclaimed our faction as Trotsky's faction.

We worked for about six months here without any communication with him until he was deported to Turkey—Constantinople—and then we established communication with him by mail. Later, various leading members of the party visited him. We had very extensive correspondence with him, and in this correspondence and in visits by individual members, we had an extremely close relation to him and regarded him all the time as the theoretical inspirer and teacher of our movement.

Q: When did you first visit Trotsky?

A: I visited him in France in 1934—that is, for the first time after our expulsion from the Communist Party.

Q: And what role, if any, did Trotsky play in formulating the doctrines of the Socialist Workers Party?

A: He played a very important role. Although he did not write our party documents, his ideas interpreting Marxism in our time were the source from which we got our main concepts and rewrote them in American terms, tried to apply them to American conditions.

Q: Did he write any articles about conditions and developments in the United States in those days?

A: I don't recall that he wrote much in those days about America.

Q: Did he at any time in those days tell you as to what practical action should be taken in the United States by your group?

A: Yes. One of the subjects of controversy in our early days was what kind of activity we should occupy ourselves with.

He supported the idea of a purely propagandistic activity in our early days—that is, as distinguished from what we call mass work. We were so few in numbers, we could not hope to do anything except to try to publish a paper and convert some people to our basic ideas; a very, very modest task of routine propaganda was assigned by the necessity of the situation to our group at that time, and he supported that.

Q: When did you first make frequent contact with Trotsky?

A: He was driven out of France and then out of Norway and finally received asylum in Mexico by the action of President Cardenas. If I am correct as to the exact month, I think it was January 1937.

Thereafter he lived in Mexico until August 21, 1940, when he was assassinated. In the period that he was there we made frequent visits to him. I personally was there to see him twice, once in the spring of 1938 and again in the summer of 1940. Other party leaders and party members visited him frequently. I personally maintained a very active correspondence with him, and so did other members of the party, and I would say we were in very, very intimate contact with him after he came to Mexico.

Q: What did the Socialist Workers Party do with reference to helping Trotsky guard himself, and also with reference to aiding him in his expenses?

A: We knew that Trotsky was marked for assassination by Stalin, who had killed off practically all the important leaders of the revolution through his mass trials and his purges and frame-ups and so forth. We knew that Trotsky, as the greatest of all the opponents of Stalin, was marked for assassination, and we undertook to protect him. We set up a special committee which had the sole purpose of collecting funds to support this endeavor.

We supplied guards, we supplied money regularly and systematically for transforming his house into as close to a fortress as possible. We collected and supplied the funds to buy the house for him. We supplied the expenses of the guards who were sent there, and in general, in every way possible extended ourselves to protect his life and facilitate his work.

Q: What was the nature of the discussions that you held with Trotsky while you were there?

A: All the important problems of the world movement.

Q: Any problems of the American labor movement?

A: Yes.

Q: Did you ever discuss the question of union defense guards and Local 544 with him?

A: No, I personally had no discussion with him about 544 defense guards. We discussed with him the question of defense guards in general. This, I think, was in our visit in 1938.

Q: Do you know of your own knowledge whether Trotsky had many visitors?

A: Yes, I know that he did. I know that he had many visitors, because in my capacity as secretary of the party I frequently was called upon to give letters of introduction to people who wanted to visit him. He was visited, not only by our members, but by journalists, by school teachers, a history class which used to tour Mexico, and he was visited by public people of many kinds and opinions while he was there.

Q: Then the discussions that you had with Trotsky referred and related to general political questions, did they not?

A: Yes—questions of the war, of fascism, trade unionism—

Q: But they had nothing to do with party activities, branches or of particular sections of the party?

A: No, I don't recall that Trotsky ever interested himself in the detailed local work of the party; I don't recall that.

Q: How busy a man was he?

A: He was the busiest man I ever knew. Trotsky, in addition to all his political work and his enormous correspondence, and his journalistic work—and he wrote innumerable articles and pamphlets for us—he wrote for magazines and newspapers, such as *The New York Times, Saturday Evening Post, Liberty* and other magazines—and in addition to that, he produced, in the eleven years since his exile to Turkey in 1929 to his death in 1940, a literary output greater by volume than that of the average writer who does nothing else but write.

He wrote the three huge volumes on the history of the Russian Revolution which, from the point of view of literary labor, could be considered a life task by any writer. He wrote a full-sized book called *The Revolution Betrayed,* and he wrote his autobiography and innumerable smaller books and pamphlets and articles in that period.

Q: The party, then, never bothered him with minor questions of policy and activities?

A: Not to my knowledge; I know I never did.

Q: Will you tell the court and jury the position of the Socialist Workers Party on workers' defense guards?

A: Well the party is in favor of the workers organizing defense guards wherever their organizations or their meetings are threatened by hoodlum violence. The workers should not permit their meetings to be broken up or their halls to be wrecked, or their work to be interfered with, by Ku Klux Klanners or Silver Shirts or fascists of any type, or hoodlums, or reactionary thugs, but should organize a guard and protect themselves where it is necessary.

Q: How long ago was the idea of a workers' defense guard first put forth by the group of which you are a member?

A: I may say that I have known about this idea, which we didn't invent at all, all my thirty years in the labor movement. I have known about the idea of workers' defense guards and seen them organized and helped to organize them more than once long before I ever heard of the Russian Revolution.

Q: And did the Trotskyist group ever start organizing these guards before it became the Socialist Workers Party?

A: Yes, in the first year of our existence, in 1929. The Communist Party, the Stalinists, tried to break up our meetings by hoodlum violence. They did break up a number of meetings and we reacted to that by organizing a workers' defense guard to protect our meetings, and invited to participate in this guard not only Trotskyists, but other workers' organizations which were also being attacked by the Stalinist hoodlums.

Let me explain this. The Stalinists had a system in those days of trying to break up meetings of the Socialist Party, of the IWW, of a group called the Proletarians, of anybody who didn't agree with the Stalinists. They tried the Stalin game of breaking them up, so in self-defense, without any theory from anybody, we reacted by organizing workers' defense guards to protect our meetings. And I may add, parenthetically, we protected them so well that we put a stop to that monkey business at the cost of a few cracked heads, which I personally greatly appreciated in those days.

Q: I show you a volume of the *Militant,* marked 1928 and 1930, and ask that you refresh your recollection from that volume, and tell the jury on what occasions workers' defense guards were organized by the Trotskyist group. Just read the item, and then tell the jury, without reading the item to the jury.

A: The first one is dated January 1, 1929. It refers to a meeting addressed by me in New Haven, Connecticut, under the title, "The Truth About Trotsky and the Platform of the Opposition." It is a news account of the meeting.

Q: Well, Mr. Cannon, just read that and then tell the jury what you remember about that incident.

A: I remember it very well, because they sent a gang of hoodlums to the meeting and they broke it up and didn't permit me to continue my speech, and created a fight, and in the midst of the fight the police came to the hall and declared the meeting dissolved. That is a report of a meeting in the Labor Lyceum at New Haven, Connecticut, December 21, 1928.

Q: And did you subsequently organize any defense guards to protect your meetings?

A: Yes, in the same account is the report of a second meeting held in Philadelphia on December 27, with Max Schactman as the speaker and it states there that, profiting by the experience in New Haven, they organized a workers' defense guard which came and protected the meeting, and the speaker was allowed to continue without disruption.

Q: Did you ever hold a meeting where you spoke where workers' defense guards protected the meeting?

A: Yes. Here is the *Militant* (indicating) under date of January 15, 1929, which reports a meeting addressed by me in Cleveland, Ohio, on the same subject about which I was speaking then, "The Truth About Trotsky and the Russian Opposition," and the account in the paper tells about a gang of Stalinists who came there and tried to disrupt the meeting, and heckled the speaker, and they began to try violence—

Q: You were the speaker, were you?

A: I was the speaker, and I recall very well that I was protected by a guard which we had organized, and the report says that the workers' guard finally formed a flying wedge and put the disrupters out of the meeting, and the speaker was allowed to continue to the end.

Q: And subsequent to that, did you ever speak at meetings where workers' defense guards were organized to protect those meetings?

A: Yes, here is a report in the *Militant* of February 1929, and it tells about two meetings addressed by me in the city of Minneapolis.

Q: And do you remember what happened at those meetings?

A: Yes, the first meeting we attempted to hold in some lodge hall here—I forget the name, AOUW Hall, it is reported here— I recall at this meeting, before the meeting started, a gang of Stalinist hoodlums invaded the meeting and attacked Oscar Coover with blackjacks, where he was standing at the door taking tickets, I think, and forced their way into the hall before the crowd had come, got front seats, and then as the crowd came in and I went to the front and tried to speak, they got up and interfered and heckled and disturbed and disrupted the meeting until it finally ended in a free-for-all scuffle, and I didn't get a chance to make my speech. Then this account here tells—

Q: Well, what do you remember?

A: Yes, it is reported here in this issue of the paper that we then went to the IWW Hall here—that is another radical organization which we are not affiliated with, but who had also suffered from these Stalinist tactics, and asked them if they would cooperate with us in organizing a guard to protect the meeting, so that I could speak on the subject that I was touring the country then on, "The Truth About Trotsky and Our Platform." They agreed.

We formed a workers' defense guard in Minneapolis in January 1929, and the IWW gave us the use of their hall. They had a hall of their own somewhere down here on Washington Street. We advertised the meeting widely and announced that this meeting was going to be held under the protection of the workers' guard. And I personally know that there was such a guard, that they equipped themselves with hatchet handles, and stood along the side of the hall, and stood out in front and announced that nobody should interfere with this meeting. I spoke for about two hours there without any interference, under the protection of that workers' guard.

Q: So that you can say from your knowledge that the workers' defense guard—

A: There are more news accounts here, if you want them. That was a period until we finally established our right to be let alone, and then there was no more need for the guard, and we dissolved.

Q: Now, with reference to the workers' defense guard advocated by the Socialist Workers Party, what formal action did the party take at any time?

A: Well, in this later period of 1938 and '39, in some parts of the country we were confronted with an incipient fascist movement. Different organizations with different names began preaching Hitlerite doctrines in this country, and tried to practice Hitlerite methods of physical intimidation of workers' meetings, of Jews, Jewish stores, and suppressing free speech by violent methods.

In New York it became a rather acute problem. The various Bundists and associated groups in New York developed the practice of breaking up street meetings when either our party or some other workers' party would attempt to speak under a permit given by the city authorities. They had a habit of going around and molesting Jewish storekeepers, picketing them, and beating them, and challenging them to fight, and so on.

There was an organization rampant at that time called the "Silver Shirts." I don't recall them in New York, but at various points in the West and Midwest.

Q: Do you recall the Christian Front?

A: Yes, in New York the Bundists and the Christian Front, and two or three other would-be fascist organizations, used to combine on this kind of business. At this time free speech was being very flagrantly denied in Jersey City under the authority of this man Hague who announced that he was the law, got the habit of chasing people out of town and permitting meetings to be broken up ostensibly not by the authorities, but by the "outraged citizens" whom he and his gang had organized for that purpose. In general there were signs then—there was a lot of discontent and unrest in the country—there were signs of a fascist movement growing up, and the question arose of how we could protect, not only ourselves, but how could the unions protect themselves. For example, in Jersey City picketing was denied by these means and the right to strike infringed upon—very serious questions of the invasion of civil liberties by unofficial bodies.

Basing ourselves on the experiences of the German and Italian fascist movements, which began with gangs of hoodlums and ended by destroying completely the labor unions and all workers' organizations and all civil rights—we came to the conclusion that the fascists should be met on their own ground, and that we should raise the slogan of workers' defense guards to protect workers' meetings, halls and institutions against hoodlum violence by the incipient fascists.

We discussed that with Trotsky; his part in it was primarily an exposition of the development of the fascist movement in Europe. I don't recall now whether he originated the idea, but at any rate he heartily seconded it that our party should propose that the unions, wherever their peace was menaced by these hoodlums, should organize workers' defense guards and protect themselves.

q: And did the unions follow the advice of the party?

a: I recall that we organized, in cooperation with some other radicals and some Jewish people—even some Jewish nationalists who didn't agree with our socialist program, but agreed on defending their human rights to live—we formed at that time a workers' defense guard in New York. To protect not only the meetings of our party but of any organization menaced by these hoodlums. To protect citizens from molestation in the Bronx, where these hoodlums were intimidating and insulting Jewish people. This guard had several scuffles and fights with these gangs.

Then conditions in the country began to change. The economic situation in the country improved a bit. The question of the European war began to absorb attention, and take it away from these provincial American Hitlers. The fascist movement dropped into passivity and our workers' defense guard in New York didn't have anything to do and it just passed out of existence. In Los Angeles, if I recall correctly, there was a similar experience.

q: Did any international trade unions ever adopt that idea, as far as you know?

a: I don't know. I know the question was raised in the Garment Workers Union, which had a double concern about the matter because, first, as a labor union they were menaced by the growth of fascism, and second, a large percentage of their members are Jews who are considered proper victims by these hoodlums. A resolution was passed in favor of the idea in one of the garment locals in New York, and was referred then to the International Executive Board for consideration, and some correspondence and some interviews between our comrades who had sponsored the idea and the officers of the International Ladies' Garment Workers Union took place. I don't think it developed any further, either positively or negatively, because the fascist movement subsided and the issue got cold.

Q: So that the issue of the workers' defense guard died down because a change of conditions occurred?

A: Yes. We retained the proposal for workers' defense guards in our program. I believe it is on the editorial page of the *Militant* as one of the points we are proposing as a practical program.

Q: And it becomes vital especially in view of a possible fascist movement in our country?

A: Yes. At that time our paper was full of stories and articles about the Bundists and the Christian Fronters, and so on, but if you look over the files, they show a gradual recession of reports about fascist violence. And the question of the workers' defense guard left the pages of the paper and is only occasionally raised there now in a slogan.

(Defendants' Exhibit H was marked for identification.)

THE WITNESS (Continuing):—I might add, Mr. Goldman, that so far as I know, there doesn't exist now any functioning workers' defense guard in any part of the country that our members are associated with, not to my knowledge. But we retain the idea for practical education in case the unions should again encounter the experience of those days.

MR. GOLDMAN: I offer in evidence, Your Honor, Defendants' Exhibit H-1 to H-5, inclusive, being a copy of a resolution entitled "Convention Resolution on Workers' Defense Guard," published in the *Socialist Appeal* of July 7, 1939.

THE COURT: It will be received.

MR. GOLDMAN: I do not intend to read it, because the witness made an exposition of it.

You can take the witness.

THE COURT: I think we might recess at this point.

(Afternoon Recess)

Cross-Examination by Mr. Schweinhaut (Prosecutor):

Q: Now you stated on direct examination that the expropriation of private property, without compensation, was not a principle of the Socialist Workers Party, but I want to read to you from the Declaration of Principles this sentence, and ask you a question about it:

"The most important of the social economic measures to be taken by the workers' state in its initial period is the expropriation and socialization, without compensation, of all monopolies in industry and land, or mines, factories, and shipping, all public utilities, railroads, airplane systems, and other organized means of communications, all banks, credit agencies, and gold stores, and all other supplies and services that the revolutionary government finds it necessary to take over in order to lay the foundations of a socialist society."

What have you to say about that Mr. Cannon?

A: If I remember correctly, I said it is not a principle of Marxism that property taken by the government cannot be compensated for.

Q: Are you quite certain you were discussing Marxism as distinguished from the program of the party at the time?

A:. I think I referred to Marxist authorities. I had in mind particularly the authority of Trotsky.

Q: Well, in any event it is a principle of the Socialist Workers Party that such property shall be taken without compensation?

A: That is in the Declaration. But it is not a principle.

Q: Would you mind explaining why the present owners of the property, who have acquired their ownership, at least, by constitutional means, would be given nothing for it? Why is that principle embodied in the program of the party?

A: The Sixty Families who own the bulk of the industries and banks of America are not rightfully entitled to so much ownership and power over the lives of the people who produced this property by their labor.

Q: You would give them, then, no credit for their own industry and effort, education, intelligence—

A: Yes, I would give them the same credit that every citizen will have who participates in the production of the wealth of the country—that is, the opportunity to function in the new society on the basis of equality.

Q: Yes. But I am talking about the time when you take the power and with it the property, as of that time you would take it over without any compensation, and I ask you therefore, why you do not at that time take into account the effort, the industry, the intelligence, and I might add, the risk of loss, that has been constantly present, of those people?

A: What we are concerned with is the welfare of the great mass of the people. Their welfare categorically requires that the productive plants of this country be transferred from private hands into the hands of the public. That is what we are concerned with first of all. Industry must be nationalized— private property must be eliminated in the industrial process. The question of the rights and the interests of the comparatively small number of the population who are affected by that drastic measure is naturally secondary to what we consider this public necessity, public interest.

I don't see any principled reason why such people, who are deprived of their ability or their power to exploit labor any more, cannot be given consideration on condition that they acquiesce in the will of the majority. They can be pensioned, they can be given consideration in view of their age, or their incapacity for labor, or their agreement not to resist by force the mandate of the majority.

As a matter of fact I think we would be in favor of that.

Q: You would give them a pension?

A: Possibly, yes.

Q: Well, now, is it your theory that no person who has acquired large property holdings could have done it in other ways than by the exploitation of the workers?

A: That is the way property is created under capitalism.

Q: Now, will you please tell us what you mean by "exploitation"?

A: That means the employment of wage labor at a rate of pay less than the value of the product of the labor.

Q: Well, then, it is an arbitrary dogma, shall we say, of the Socialist Workers Party that no person who labors is adequately paid under this present system of government?

A: I wouldn't say "no person." Some people are very badly overpaid.

Q: I am talking about the workers—the same workers you are talking about.

A: Yes, I can conceive of even a worker being overpaid—that is, an unproductive, an unskillful or negligent worker.

But when we speak of wage labor we speak of the average, and the general rule. Marxism deals in the general and not in the analysis of each and every individual worker. The workers, taken collectively and an average struck, produce an enormous amount of wealth for which they do not receive the equivalent in wages. That is surplus value, according to Marxist terminology. That is profit that goes into the hands of the capitalists, not in return for labor but as profit on investment.

Q: And you think they should have no profit on their investment?

A: We want to eliminate the whole profit system. We want to have production for use, not for profit.

Q: Well, now, you would expropriate the property, not only of the Sixty Families, but of anyone who owns property in a large measure, is that correct?

A: Our program specifically excludes the expropriation or interference with small proprietors. We speak of people who have big holdings and exploit labor. Their property shall be transferred to the ownership and control of the public as represented by the workers' and farmers' government.

Q: Where did the term "Sixty Families" originate?

A: To my knowledge, it first came to public attention through a book written by a brilliant journalist named Ferdinand Lundberg.

Four or five years ago Mr. Lundberg conducted researches into the ownership and control of American industry, banks, and so forth. Out of an exhaustive research he produced a remarkably documented book entitled *America's Sixty Families,* in which he set out facts and figures to prove that the decisive control of American industry, banks and other institutions which represent the real economic wealth and power of this country—that this is concentrated in the ownership and control of sixty families whom he listed.

Mr. Lundberg's work, as far as I know, has never been seriously controverted. I recall that even such a representative figure of the present administration as Secretary Ickes spoke on the radio and referred to this book as authority for some position he was taking in a current political dispute.

Q: Now, then, you have used the term—when you use it in the party literature—literally then, have you not, having specific reference to sixty specific families?

A: I wouldn't say it is an ironclad literal description. It is an approximation of the real situation. We don't propose to limit the thing exactly to that, but the expression "Sixty Families" graphically illustrates what has been happening in the country. While the workers were working and the farmers were farming, Sixty Families were getting control of the country, and it is a very graphic figure to use in our agitation. A lot of people don't realize what has been going on in the concentration of wealth in this country.

Q: Let me ask you a question or two, if you please, about the concept of an imperialist, capitalist government. You have said that the present government of the United States is both imperialist and capitalist.

A: Yes.

Q: You believe, then, that the government is the tool of the capitalists?

A: It is the representative of the capitalists.

Q: And then, in order to suppress the capitalists, should they resist you, it follows, of course, that you must suppress the government?

A: We are going to change the government.

Q: So you are going to suppress the government as a natural concomitant of the transaction of suppressing the capitalists. That is correct, isn't it?

A: After we get the majority and get the power—if that power comes into our hands by peaceful, democratic processes, in that case we will radically change the whole structure of the government, reorganizing it on a basis of council representation, as I described this morning.

Q: Well, now, suppose the government doesn't follow the example of Count Karolyi and turn it over to you. Then you are going to take it, aren't you?

A: You mean if they resist a majority in a democratic election?

Q: Oh, you are going to do it by election?

A: We are participating in elections all the time. All that we have said is that the ruling class of this country will resort to violence before there is a fair opportunity to test the majority or the minority in the democratic process.

Q: Well, now, tell us how you think that is going to come about and work out here in this country. Don't, for the purpose of that question, if you please, use the illustration of any other revolution. But how do you think it is going to work out here? Let me suggest your train of thought upon that: You say that if they resist an election, or something of that sort—tell us what you mean by that; give us the program as you envision it.

A: As things are going now, and as they conceivably can in the near future, we, as a minority party, will keep preaching our doctrines, recruiting members, doing our best to grow bigger, more popular, and get more support.

Naturally, if we have to rely solely on the effectiveness of our arguments, things remaining as they are, we will not grow very fast; but we, as Marxists, believe that historical development will come powerfully to the aid of our ideas. Continued bankruptcy of the present system, its inability to solve its problems, its worsening of the conditions of the people, will push them on the road in search of a solution of what seems to them an absolutely hopeless situation.

Under those conditions our program can appear to the people more and more plausible, more and more reasonable, and we can begin to become a stronger party. It has happened before with parties of similar ideas.

Q: I understand now; you are doing all right. But understand that I want you to tell us how you think it is going to work out in this country.

A: As our party grows, it in itself will be a reflection of the growth and development of the broad labor movement, the trade unions. The unions will be pushed more and more along the lines of aggressive action, because the capitalists of America don't think the workers are entitled to decent living and decent hours and will try to squeeze the workers down.

The capitalists will try to use the pretext of "national defense" and the war danger to deprive the workers of the right to strike. And once they have deprived the workers of the right to strike on so-called patriotic pretexts, then the capitalists will begin squeezing down wages and refusing concessions, and pushing the workers on the road to a more radical attitude toward the state of affairs, and our party will grow with that.

The next thing that will probably appear on the horizon is attempts of these Sixty Families and their supporters to stop the popularizing of ideas inimical to the capitalists, and to check by legislation the organization of the workers. You have the beginning of it here in Minnesota with the Stassen Anti-Strike Law.

They will begin arresting people for expressing their honest opinions, and putting them in jail, framing them up. They will begin organizing bands of fascist hoodlums as, in Germany, Fritz Thyssen, the big steel magnate, confessed that he gave millions of marks to finance the organization of Hitler's hoodlums. The task of Hitler's hoodlums was to go around breaking up workers' meetings, and by violent assaults depriving the workers of their civil liberties and democratic rights.

Q: The capitalists will use legislation?

A: Yes, legislation violating the First Amendment of the Constitution which prohibits this kind of legislation.

And in this situation they will go through the war. They won't stop with any army of a million and a half; they will organize an army of five million. They will send millions of American boys abroad for imperialist war adventures to protect their markets and their profits. Lives will be lost. Conditions at home will grow worse, because all this sixty to one hundred billions of dollars that they are appropriating for the wasteful expenses of war has got to be paid for by somebody and they will try to make the masses and the poor farmers pay it.

Misery will grow and increase, and demands will grow in this country, among people who want freedom and a right to live, for some way out of this madhouse of war and unemployment and growing fascism.

Q: Will this be during the war now, this part in your story?

A: Well, it can happen during the war, if the war is prolonged. Or it can happen in a catastrophically rapid manner at the end of the war, when millions of men return home from victories or defeats, as the case may be, to find no jobs waiting for them, and the whole economic prosperity of the day is exploded because it is based on the production of armaments.

The moment they stop building battleships and bombers and guns and ammunition, and all the other implements of war, you will have an army of fifteen to twenty-five million unemployed in this country. The small businessmen will be ruined and the farmers who have been in a chronic crisis for twenty-five years will have still worsened conditions.

The people of this country are going to begin thinking seriously then about finding some kind of a political solution for this crisis that the present leaders got them into and can't get them out of. That is the way I visualize the development.

What do we want then? We want the simple right to advocate our ideas. We want the right to have free speech and free press and free assemblage.

Q: I know, but I think you are getting a little bit off the track. You have gotten to the point now in your story of how it is going to come about in the United States where everybody is pretty unhappy about the situation, or maybe worse than unhappy—angry. Go on from there and tell us—what is the next step?

A: That is what I intend to do. I said, what do we want in that situation?

We want the opportunity to continue explaining to the people of America what our plan is to solve this problem.

That is what we want, and granted that demand, we will put our program forward in elections. We will introduce resolutions in unions. We will introduce resolutions in farmers' organizations. We will try to bring about conferences between the workers in the cities and the farmers, to see if we can work out a joint program to propose a solution.

We will participate in elections, and if we are elected and are not deprived of our electoral rights, we will begin debating the question in Congress. Given this one small provision, that we retain our constitutional rights, we have every reason to be confident that we can win over the majority of the people to our program.

And the question of whether the will of this majority will be asserted in an orderly and democratic manner is not going to be determined by us; that is going to be determined by your Sixty Families, whether they want to begin the violence, or whether they want to accept a peaceful solution.

Q: Wait a minute. You haven't gotten yourself elected to control of the government yet. You are just at a point where maybe you have won an election or two. You contemplate that you will be able to elect yourself into control of the government?

A: I think it is conceivable, yes.

Q: I mean, that is what you seek? That is your aim?

A: That is the purpose in having candidates, to get them elected.

Q: Do you believe you can accomplish the control or acquisition, shall we say, of governmental power by being elected to it?

A: We can accomplish it if we are not interfered with by violence on the part of the capitalists.

Q: You mean, the capitalists are not going to let you be elected?

A: When we say that it is an illusion to expect that we can effect the social transformation by parliamentary action, that doesn't mean that we don't want to do it, or that we wouldn't gladly accept such a method. We don't believe, on the basis of our knowledge of history, and on the basis of our knowledge of the greed and rapacity of the American ruling class, that they will permit that kind of solution.

Q: Then let's go back to the question that I asked you. You don't believe that the capitalists, the Sixty Families and what not, will permit you to be elected to power?

A: No.

Q: How are they going to stop you from doing that—won't they let the people vote?

A: They can stop it in various ways.

Q: How are they going to do that?

A: They can abrogate elections.

Q: Tell us about that, please.

A: That has been done, you know, so many times and in so many countries, that there is nothing novel about it.

Q: How are they going to do that?

A: By cancelling elections; and you know, we are not the only ones who anticipate such possibilities.

Q: You mean, they are just not going to permit any elections to be held?

A: Even such a public figure as Lindbergh has raised the question seriously whether there will be congressional elections permitted in 1942. I think he is ahead of time, but it is not necessarily a Trotskyist idea that they will stop elections.

Q: Possibly I haven't made myself clear. I am trying to find out now, how the capitalists are going to prevent you from being elected into office? You said there were several ways they could do that. One of them is to abrogate elections. Now, I ask you what you mean by that? Do you mean that the capitalists will not permit any elections at all to be held?

A: That is possible, yes.

Q: Is that one way you think you are going to be prevented from being elected into office?

A: That is one way, yes; that has been done.

Q: Here?

A: Not here yet, no. In France, the Petain government wasn't elected and doesn't permit any elections to test it. They put an end to the democratic parliament. I personally think that—

THE COURT: I think, Mr. Cannon, you ought to stick to the text suggested by the question. We are not interested in elections in France at this stage of the proceeding.

Q: (By Mr. Schweinhaut): Now, I don't want to prolong this, but I do want you to try to answer me. I want to know again how the capitalists in the United States of America are going to prevent you from being elected into office? Now, you have answered one of the several ways. They are going to stop elections from being held at all.

A: Yes.

Q: Tell us what other ways they are going to prevent you from being elected into office.

A: Another way is to pass discriminatory legislation, penalizing workers' parties.

Q: Explain that, please.

A: Restricting the functioning of workers' parties, preventing their full freedom of action, which would be necessary to secure parliamentary victories.

Q: And any other ways?

A: Yes. Another way, the most likely way for the Sixty Families, is to organize and subsidize a fascist movement with the aim of destroying the labor movement by force before it has an opportunity to test its strength in elections.

That is the way it was done in Italy; and I would like to explain that I am only using these references to other countries because they throw light on the process that is possible here. It was not my intention to bring in these examples as an extraneous issue. We think capitalist society operates in one country or another according to similar laws under similar conditions.

Q: Now, how are you going to prevent those things from happening? You want to stop them before they happen, I assume?

A: Yes.

Q: How are you going to do that?

A: First of all, we are going to try to assert our rights. We are going to try our best to get the support of enough people, whether they agree with our political theory or not, to maintain the democratic processes and civil rights of all the population. We are going to try to do that.

When we see fascist bands organizing with the aim of breaking up the labor movement, we are going to advise the workers, before it is too late, to organize workers' defense guards and not permit the fascist hoodlums to break up workers' organizations and meetings.

Those are two of the most important and immediate ideas we have about protecting the rights of the workers and their possibilities to develop their movement in a democratic process.

Q: Now suppose there is no abrogation of elections. You are going to continue to propagandize only, is that correct?

A: That is right.

Q: To try to get yourselves elected into office?

A: That is right.

Q: No matter how long it takes?

A: We can't determine the time at all.

Q: Now how do you expect the capitalists to abrogate the elections? How will they accomplish that purpose?

A: They can do it in various ways—by decree, by vote of Congress declaring there is a state of emergency which requires dispensing with election struggles, and handing the power over to the president or somebody to rule for this period, which may be long or short—but most likely it would be long.

That is precisely what was done to a legally constituted parliament elected by the suffrage of the French people, containing representatives of various parties—Socialists, Radical Socialist, Conservative, Communist and other parties. This parliament was dissolved, and a dictator appointed with power to rule the country at his will until further notice. That is what happened just like that (indicating).

Q: Supposing they don't do those things that you anticipate, and you get yourself elected into control of the government, control of the Senate and the House, let us say, and you elect a president, too. Do you expect then that the army and navy are going to turn against you and try to resist your authority?

A: I anticipate that some of the officers would—those who

are tied most closely to the upper circles of the ruling class. I would expect some of them to attempt to dispute the authority of the people's government. That happened in other instances.

Q: Yes, I know you are illustrating by that. I am talking about this country. You have got yourself elected into control of the government now. Now tell us how you expect the resistance against your authority is going to be made. Who is going to do it, and how is it going to be done?

A: It would be done by the agents of the ruling class that is facing dispossession.

Q: Do you expect the army and navy of the United States government to turn its guns against you when you are in duly elected control of the government?

A: Yes, I would expect some of the officers to do it—not all of them. If all of the army and navy would be of such a mind, it would be manifestly impossible to be elected in the first place, because the army and navy are more or less in their ranks reflective of the general population, and if we are elected by a majority vote, you can be sure that our popularity in the masses of the people will be reflected in the military establishment. That is always the case.

Q: Well, how would you resist this uprising against you?

A: The same way Lincoln did in 1861.

Q: Would you already have an army, or would you use the army that you find standing when you came into power?

A: We will just use what measures are possible. A good section of the American army and it best officers in 1861 revolted against the authority of the legally elected government of Lincoln. Lincoln took what he could and recruited some more and gave them a fight, and I always thought it was a wonderfully good idea.

Q: But in the meanwhile you want to build, do you not, a workers' militia?

A: A workers' defense guard, yes.

Q: I mean, not alone for the purpose of defending the union halls, but for other purposes, isn't that right? Don't you want to build, while you are advancing toward power, a workers' militia? To help you when you get into power?

A: We use the expression "workers' defense guards" because that is most American and most easily and precisely defines what we want. The workers' defense guards will grow in size and strength insofar as the guards have a task to perform, not because we want them to grow.

If the fascists grow and fight the unions, the unions must inevitably counter that movement by developing their defense guards, and if the defense guards are overpowered by fascist gangsters and hoodlums and thugs, the only answer of the unions can be to strengthen the guards, and in the course of that struggle between the fascist gangs and the workers' defense guards, we hope the workers' defense guards will grow strong and eventually become a very effective power.

Q: Well, let's sort of boil the thing down a little bit. You do not expect that you will be able to be elected into office, do you?

A: No, our program says we do not expect that, and for the reasons that I have given you.

Q: But you expect to take power, nevertheless, do you not?

A: Yes, the revolution can't be stopped by suppression, because the revolution is a tremendous social movement of great masses of people.

Q: So your party looks forward to an inevitable civil war brought about by the difference between your views and those of the capitalists?

A: If you will permit me, I would like to say we don't look forward to it in the sense of wanting it.

Q: I understand you, yes.

A: And we don't consider it inevitable. A variation of historical processes is possible.

But we say the overwhelming weight of possibility, based upon historical experience, is that the ruling class of this country will attempt to resolve the conflict with the workers by fascist violence before we gain a majority in Congress. Or if it should come to the point where we gain a majority in a democratic election, the ruling class would stage a slaveholders' rebellion against it. And we will undertake to put down that rebellion as decisively as possible.

Q: And to that end you want to start in advance to build up a workers' army, don't you?

A: You can't by mere program build up a workers' army to confront such a thing. The force of the workers will grow up out of their unions, out of their workers' defense guards, out of the rank and file of the soldiers and the farmers who are in the armed forces, who will not support the slaveholders' rebellion. We will not be without resources if we have a majority of the people.

Q: I understand that. Now, the setting up of union defense guards in all trade unions would be very beneficial to your program if the resistance you anticipate occurs, wouldn't it?

A: It will be an absolutely indispensable thing, yes.

Q: So that it is a good idea for your ultimate purposes to have union defense guards right now?

A: It is a good idea, if you can organize them. But you cannot organize workers' defense guards merely because you want them—only when there is a pressing need for them that is obvious to the workers, regardless of their agreement with our ideas.

Q: It would be a pleasing thing, would it not, to the Socialist Workers Party to be able to establish workers' guards in all trade unions for the ultimate purpose of the party?

A: I would go further than that and say that the establishment of workers' defense guards is an almost automatic process as the unions encounter the violence of fascist hoodlums. Our task will be to accelerate it, to say it is a good idea, build it up and make it stronger and don't let the fascists break up your movement and drive you into slavery.

But the guard is not something we can suck out of our fingers. It is a natural process growing out of the development of the struggle and we try to see it in advance, try to accelerate it, try to popularize the idea, convince the workers it is a good thing, and bestir themselves about it.

But no matter how many books we write, or how much we holler, we couldn't organize a workers' defense guard in any place where a union is operating uninterfered with. That is illustrated, you may say, by way of Minneapolis where we have very good friends and influential comrades in the unions—but when the Silver Shirt menace disappeared, the union defense guard just didn't find any function, and dropped into quiescence. It can't be built artificially.

Q: Are you saying that the union defense guard doesn't exist any longer?

A: I don't know whether it exists formally, but it doesn't function, as far as I was able to judge from the testimony.

Q: Now, let me ask you this question: After you get into power, you are going to establish an army, aren't you?

A: Eventually, yes.

Q: Your Declaration of Principles says the workers' state will not have a professional army, but will depend upon a mass workers' militia in which distinctions other than those required for technical efficiency will be abolished and democratic control over officers will be exercised by the ranks.

A: That has always been the Marxist conception of an army.

Q: Well now, would you mind elaborating on that a little bit?

A: We want to do away with professional soldiers. The workers' state would probably for some time need a military establishment even if it came to an agreement with the dispossessed capitalists here to pension them off in return for their submission to the decision of the majority. There is the possibility that a capitalist Europe, a Hitler or something like that, would menace our country, and we would have to maintain a military establishment to defend the country.

Our idea is not to have a professional soldier class except, of course, in technical competence. Every able-bodied citizen would be liable for military service, alternately. The people should be armed.

Q: I think I probably understand that, but specifically will you tell us what this means (reading from the Declaration of Principles): "in which distinctions other than those required for technical efficiency will be abolished and democratic control over officers will be exercised by the ranks." Let's take the first one: "distinctions other than those required for technical efficiency will be abolished." What does that mean?

A: There have to be certain people in the military establishment who are proficient in certain techniques—artillery, aircraft, and so on.

The distinctions that we want abolished are the distinctions of privilege in the army, the distinctions which make it possible for the officers to have greater compensations than the soldier, and not only greater, but so far greater that the officer lives in a different world. It is possible for the officer to marry, to have a social life, to live something like a human being; while the soldier, because of his low wages, is deprived of these possibilities.

If we had our way, we would abolish these distinctions of privilege and secure to every member of the military apparatus a more or less similar compensation, regulation of privileges, and so on. Of course, I don't say that applies only to the army. That applies to society in general, in our theory.

Q: The private would be equal to the major general under that theory, in all respects, to use an extreme basis, I suppose?

A: Equal not in his military knowledge—equal not in his military position, but equal in his right to have a decent living and social life. Why shouldn't he?

Q: I am asking you. Take the captain, would he be able to give orders to his privates?

A: Yes.

Q: Would they have to take the orders?

A: Yes, you can't have a military establishment without discipline, without command.

Q: What do you mean by "control over officers exercised by the ranks"?

A: We are in favor of the ranks having the privilege of electing their officers in the military establishment, the same way they have the privilege of electing their city officials in civil life, or their union officials in the unions. We believe that on the whole they would get a better grade of officers, and ones in whom they would put more confidence, than by having officers imposed upon them. You will get a better discipline because of the democratic right granted to the rank and file to select their officers.

Q: Now, will you have a sort of political commissar, if that is the proper word, which would have control over the officers in the army?

A: That all depends on whether the officers are considered reliable or not.

Q: They had it, I believe, did they not, in Soviet Russia?

A: Yes, in the army after the revolution they had a lot of officers trained in the czarist regime.

Q: Would that be what you mean by democratic control of the officers?

A: No, that is an entirely different thing. By democratic control of the officers, we mean the right of the ranks to elect them and to recall them.

Q: But would you have any representative of the state administrative office, or whatever you call it, with the troops, and in control of the officers?

A: You are speaking of the institution of commissars in the Russian army?

Q: I don't know whether I am or not. I am asking you.

A: I will explain that, but that is a different point. In the reconstituted army, organized by Trotsky after the revolution, they naturally had to rely on tens of thousands of officers who had been trained under the czarist regime. The workers had had no chance to train any of their people to be officers. Many officers rallied to the support of the Soviet government, for various reasons. Some of them became converted to the revolution. Others remained hostile to the revolution but were patriotic to the country, and were willing to fight to defend it against the interventionists. Others reconciled themselves to reality, and made the best of it.

But many of them, naturally, were considered politically unreliable. The control exercised by commissars over them was not a control from the ranks such as we propose by election. This was control from the top of the government. The commissar was appointed as a trusted representative of the central government to work with the officer and see that he conducted himself loyally. That is what was worked out in life in the Russian experience.

We haven't even mentioned it in our program, because we don't know what will happen here.

I should add that insofar as these officers became assimilated into the new regime, and new officers were trained, the necessity for the commissar over the officer of doubtful loyalty was eliminated, and to that extent the institution was reduced.

Q: I would like to know whether or not having those political commissars is embraced within the program of the Socialist Workers Party?

A: No, I don't think it is stated in our program.

Q: I am asking you.

A: No, it is neither incorporated nor rejected. It is one of numerous ideas that remain to be answered.

Q: They had the same system in the Spanish Civil War recently, didn't they?

A: To some extent they did, yes.

Q: Will you explain to us a little bit, or use the Spanish Civil War as an illustration of the desirability of your own program that there be training under trade-union control and that sort of thing? Will you elaborate on that for us a little bit?

A: I mentioned that the People's Front coalition secured a majority in the elections. The reactionary minority then revolted and started a rebellion by armed force, taking with them a considerable section of the staff of the army. On the other hand, as is nearly always the case, a section of the staff remained loyal to the legally constituted government, as was the case here in our Civil War—there was a division in the army.

The workers previously had clamored for arms, but the People's Front government had refused to give them arms, and delayed so long that the workers hadn't acquired any training in the use of arms. That is one of the reasons for the victory of fascism in Spain.

The workers' organizations were the most aggressive opponents of the fascists. Our party in Spain, while it did not give political support to the People's Front government, did support and participate in the military struggle to beat back the fascists, fought in the army side by side with the republicans and democrats and so on.

The unions and workers' organizations found that they could organize and equip and put men in the field far better through their own machinery than they could through the People's Front government. The powerful unions there organized their own regiments. The political parties organized their own regiments, and they were incorporated in the fighting lines side by side with the republicans and the official forces, and fought together. Without them, a serious military struggle wouldn't have been possible in Spain. If the workers of Spain had had opportunity for military training in the previous years, particularly had they had a chance to train men to be officers, I think it is quite possible that the military outcome in Spain would have been different.

Q: Let me ask you this: The Loyalist army during the war had adopted, had it not, a theory of democratic control over officers and election of officers somewhat like that advocated by your party?

A: I believe to a certain extent that prevailed at first in some of the regiments controlled by the unions. Whether it prevailed in the army as a whole, I don't really know. I am not acquainted with sufficient intimacy with the military side of the Spanish Civil War to know that.

Q: Your party believes that the present army of the United States should be run that way, doesn't it?

A: Yes, we believe the ranks should have the right to elect their officers.

Q: Right now?

A: Right now.

Q: And in the event we get into war?

A: Yes, all the more so then, because then it is all the more important to the ranks of the soldiers to have officers that they want and that they can trust because they are going into dangerous situations. It is a very, very unhappy business to be sent into danger of one's life under officers who are not trusted.

Q: Your party members are instructed, are they not, to continue to be faithful to the party principles and theories after they are inducted into the army?

A: They are not instructed, but it is taken for granted that a man who is educated in our movement never forsakes his principles under any circumstances.

MR. SCHWEINHAUT: Would Your Honor be willing to suspend at this point?

THE COURT: Ladies and gentlemen of the jury, tomorrow is Thanksgiving Day, and we shall observe it. I hope you have a pleasant day and a comfortable one.

You will please keep in mind the admonitions of the court.

We will recess now until ten o'clock on Friday morning.

(Whereupon, at 4:35 o'clock P.M., a recess was regularly taken until 10:00 o'clock A.M., Friday, November 21, 1941.)

District Court of the United States, District of Minnesota, Fourth Division.

Friday, November 21, 1941 10:00 o'clock A.M.

James P. Cannon

one of the defendants, previously sworn, recalled, testified as follows:

Cross-Examination by Mr. Schweinhaut:

Q: Mr. Cannon, I want to read to you a clause from the *Communist Manifesto,* about which Mr. Goldman interrogated you on Friday or whenever it was: "The Communists disdain to conceal their views and aims. They openly declare that their ends can be attained only by the forcible overthrow of all existing social conditions." Does that represent the party's view or not?

A: Insofar as it is incorporated in the Declaration of Principles it does. We have interpreted that, as all other Marxist writings, in our own way, as it appears in the Declaration of Principles.

Q: You will agree, will you not, that, taken as it stands, and without anything else, it amounts to advocacy of the overthrow of the government by force?

A: No, I do not interpret it that way.

Q: You do not agree that that is what it means?

A: We do not interpret it that way, but in the Declaration of Principles—

Q: I am asking you whether or not, taking this language alone, and without anything else, do you not agree that it amounts to advocacy of the overthrow of government by force?

A: No, not necessarily because the authors of that same document, in the statement that I cited the other day, stated specifically that they thought their aims could be attained, at least in England, by the process of parliamentary democracy.

Q: Now, you know that that is not in answer to my question, don't you, Mr. Cannon? Let me ask you this, please:

Taking that language which I just read to you alone, and without anything else, don't you agree that it amounts to advocacy of overthrow of government by force?

A: No, I don't think so, because the authors themselves have interpreted it differently at least in the case of England.

Q: All right—we will let that go. When you give out the *Communist Manifesto* to your members, do you caution them against that sentence?

A: I don't know, particularly, that we do. We publish it as a historic document, ninety-three years old.

Q: You would expect the members of the party, when they read that, to understand when they read it, that it does not represent the views of the party, and that it does not advocate overthrow of government by force?

A: We expect the members of the party to be governed by the Declaration of Principles.

Q: Now, I wish to read to you from the *Founding Conference of the Fourth International,* where I find this phrase: "The strategical task of the Fourth International lies not in reforming capitalism but in its overthrow." Doesn't that mean that you do not even intend to attempt anything by legislative reformation?

A: No, it does not mean that.

Q: What does it mean?

A: On the contrary, we are constantly proposing legislative changes.

Q: What does that sentence mean to you, as found there?

A: We do not expect to attain the final aims of socialism by the reformation of capitalism which we consider an outlived system. Meanwhile, we are constantly looking out, on the road to the time when we will be able to accomplish our final aims, for suitable occasions to propose timely reforms.

Q: Isn't it a fact that throughout your literature there is constant ridicule of any idea of reforms?

A: We do not think the final aims of socialism can be accomplished by reforming a state or system which has to be replaced. But we do not consider reforms and revolution incompatible, not at all.

Q: Now, I find this line in *The Revolution of 1905* by Lenin: "It is our duty—"

MR. GOLDMAN: That was not admitted in evidence, Your Honor.

MR. SCHWEINHAUT: I am not saying it was. I want to ask the witness something about it.

Q: (Continued): "It is our duty in time of an uprising to exterminate ruthlessly all the chiefs of the civil and military authorities." Does that represent the party's views?

A: No, we have never made any such declaration.

Q: You disagree with that?

A: Yes, I don't know that that is in any way a statement of our party policy.

Q: That is part of the philosophy and dogma of Lenin with which you do not agree—is that correct?

A: We do not agree with the extermination of anybody unless it is in case of an actual armed struggle, when the rules of war apply.

Q: Then in the event that your party leads an uprising, would you agree then that the chiefs of the civil and military authorities should be exterminated ruthlessly?

A: I do not want to be made responsible, or I do not want the party made responsible, for such statements that are not in our official declarations.

Q: But you have told us that the basic views of Lenin are the basic views of the Socialist Workers Party, have you not?

A: That is right and I told you at the same time that that does not mean that we take every letter and line written by Lenin as dogma.

Q: And this is one that you do not regard as dogma, is that right?

A: Certainly not with the interpretation you give it.

Q: Let me read to you some quotations from the publication *What is Trotskyism?* designated as "Outline Course No. 2, by Jack Weber," also distributed by your party: "To realize socialism Marxism posits that it is first necessary to destroy the state machinery of the capitalist ruling class: namely, the army, the police and the state bureaucracy." And then: "The policy of Marxism remains that of utilizing the war and the arming of the workers to further the interests of the world revolution, to turn the imperialist war into civil war, to look upon the bourgeoisie at home as the main enemy." And then: "The working class cannot win power by pursuing a policy of fascism." Doesn't that mean that you and your party intend, in the forthcoming war, if we get into it, to use that means for fomenting civil war?

A: I would not put it in such a bald manner as that. I have explained here in some detail that we would continue to propagate our ideas under all circumstances, insofar as we are permitted to do so. We believe that the prolongation of the war conducted by the imperialist powers will have the inevitable effect of accelerating the decay of the system represented by the imperialist powers, of increasing the mass misery and discontent, and the demand for cessation of the slaughter, and our party will certainly undertake to offer to the public in such a situation the alternative of socialism, that is right.

Q: And you will seek to utilize war, during the war, to destroy the present form of government will you not?

A: Well, that is no secret, that we want to change this form of government.

Q: And you look forward, do you not, to the forthcoming war as the time when you may be able to accomplish that?

A: Yes, I think the forthcoming war will unquestionably weaken the imperialist governments in all countries.

Q: You said, I believe, that you will not support the war? You do not believe in national defense at all, do you?

A: Not in imperialist countries, no.

Q: I am speaking of this country.

A: I believe 100 percent in defending this country by our own means, but I do not believe in defending the imperialist governments of the world—

Q: I am speaking about the government of the United States as it is now constitutionally constituted. You do not believe in defending that, do you?

A: Not in a political sense, no.

Q: You do not believe in defending it in any sense, do you?

A: I explained the other day, that if the majority of the people decide on war, and participate in the war, our people and the people under our influence will also participate in the war. We do not sabotage the war, we do not obstruct it, but we continue to propagate our ideas, calling for a cessation of the war and calling for a change in government.

Q: Do you mean by that statement that your people, when inducted into the army, would be good soldiers?

A: Yes.

Q: And that they would seek to further the military efforts of the United States?

A: We say that our people must be good soldiers in the army, in the same sense that they are good workers in the factory, and good unionists in the union. Otherwise, they could not possibly have any influence over their comrades.

Q: How can you reconcile that statement with the statement appearing in the *Socialist Appeal* of August 1, 1939: "A Socialist who preaches national defense is a petty-bourgeois reactionary at the service of a decaying capitalism." How do you reconcile your previous answer to my question, with the statement made there?

A: We are not in favor of defending the present regime. We are opposed to the present regime.

Q: And your members who are soldiers in the army, when they are inducted into the army, will be opposed to it?

A: So far as their ideas are concerned, yes, so far as their expression of opinion is concerned, insofar as they are permitted to express their opinion.

We do not believe in capitalist authority and direction in the factory either, but as long as we are in the minority and cannot prevent it, we work in the factory, and insist that our people be good workers.

Q: And while you are working in the factory, you try to do everything you can to fight against the bosses?

A: We do everything we can in the way of explaining and propagandizing to our fellow workers the idea that it is better for them to own the factories than to be wage workers under the control of a private owner.

Q: And personally, you ridicule the idea of defending the United States government, don't you?

A: In the sense of giving political support to all forms of capitalist government, yes.

Q: I will read from one of your own speeches, and see whether that means political opposition. On November 14, 1939, in a speech of yours, you said—

A: What was the date again?

Q: November 14, 1939. This speech of yours was reported in the *Internal Bulletin,* for members only. You said: "Some comrades speak nowadays of giving 'conditional' defense to the Soviet Union. If you stop to think about it we are for conditional defense of the United States. It is so stated in the program of the Fourth International. In the event of war we will absolutely defend the country on only one small 'condition': that we first overthrow the government of the capitalists and replace it with a government of the workers." Did you mean political opposition by that?

A: I meant, that in that case we would withdraw our political opposition and become political supporters as well as military participants of the war.

Q: Do you think that statement is consistent with what I just read, which was stated by you in your speech?

A: That is what I meant by it. We have never at any time said we would not fight in the army of the United States alongside of the rest of our generation, in time of war. We said, "We will not give political support to war."

Q: Let's see whether your statement in the Declaration of Principles is consistent with what you just said: (Reading) "If, in spite of the efforts of the revolutionists and the militant workers, the U. S. government enters a new war, the S.W.P. will not under any circumstances support that war but will on the contrary fight against it. The S.W.P. will advocate the continuance of the class struggle during the war regardless of the consequences for the outcome of the American military struggle; and will try to prepare the masses to utilize the war crisis for the overthrow of U. S. capitalism and the victory of socialism." Does that mean that you are supporting the war effort?

A: No, I have never said that we support the war effort. We do not. We oppose it.

Q: And could one of your party members observe that principle and be a good soldier?

A: He could be; he not only could, but he will, in the same way that he can be a good worker in a shop while opposing wage labor in the shop. We cannot prevent it as long as we are in the minority.

Q: The Declaration of Principles also says: "The Socialist Workers Party opposes and will continue at all times to oppose every form of social-patriotism, all advocacy of 'national union' or 'suspension of the class struggle' during war time"—

A: That is under conditions of a capitalist government.

Q: You mean under the present conditions in this country today, do you not?

A: That is right.

Q: But still you say that you would not obstruct the military?

A: No, not in a military sense.

Q: I want to ask you whether what I am about to read now does not mean that you want to foment and bring about a civil war, from the pamphlet *Are You Ready for War?* published by the Fourth International, Young Peoples Socialist League: "Do we believe in turning imperialist war into civil war? This is the way by which the Russian workers secured peace in 1917 while their brothers in other lands were still struggling under the yoke of imperialism. This is the only way by which permanent peace can be gained and war abolished from the face of the earth." Doesn't that mean that you intend to foment and deliberately try to bring about civil war during the forthcoming period of war?

A: Conditions mature for the development of a revolutionary movement in wartime. We continue our opposition to the imperialist system, the imperialist regime, and try to lead it in the direction of socialism. There is no doubt whatever but what that is the aim of our party.

Q: This is from one of your convention resolutions to the same general effect, and I suppose your answer would be the same: "If the working class is unable to prevent the outbreak of war, and the United States enters directly into it, our party stands pledged to the traditional position of revolutionary Marxism. It will utilize the crisis of capitalist rule engendered by the war to prosecute the class struggle with the utmost intransigence, to strengthen the independent labor and revolutionary movement and to bring the war to a close by the revolutionary overturn of capitalism and the establishment of proletarian rule in the form of a workers' state." Is that your idea of not obstructing the military effort of this country?

A: Yes, that is a clear statement of our aims. We are going to oppose the war; we are going to speak against it.

Q: Do you suggest that this language means that you will only speak against it?

A: If you try to construe that to mean that we are going to instruct our people, or the people under our influence, to obstruct the military prosecution of the war, to break discipline, to commit sabotage, to create actions of this kind, that does not mean that. It means political opposition.

Q: Reading now from the *Manifesto of the Fourth International on the Imperialist War and the Proletarian Revolution,* I read this: "Every rank and file member of our organization is not only entitled but is duty bound to consider himself henceforth an officer in the revolutionary army which will be created in the flame of events." Do you think your members could be good soldiers and not obstruct the military effort if they obeyed that principle?

A: That does not necessarily mean officers in a military sense. When we speak of the revolutionary army, we use it in many senses. We speak of the party as the revolutionary army; we speak of the movement of the proletariat as the revolutionary army; not always in a military sense. That would not mean literally in a military sense because—

Q: I am not asking you if it does. I am asking whether one could be a good soldier in the American army and obey that principle?

A: Yes, if not, he would not have influence enough to be an officer anywhere.

Q: Let me read to you from one of your speeches on military policy, appearing in the *Socialist Appeal* of October 26, 1940: "How do we work in a conscript army, someone asked. We work the same way as in a shop. Indeed, the main purpose of industry now is supplying the army. Where would you draw the line? There is hardly an industry that won't be mobilized either for the manufacture or transportation of materials for the army. The masses are in the army, or working to supply the army. The workers are subject to military exploitation. We go in and defend the interests of the slaves of military exploitation, just as we go into the factory and fight against the capitalist exploitation there. Our basic line everywhere is the class line.

"The second point is to be careful, cautious. Make no putsches, make no premature moves that expose us and separate us from the masses. Go with the masses. Be with the masses, just as the Bolsheviks were in Kerensky's army. Why can't we do that here? And how otherwise can we do it? How otherwise, in a world dominated by militarism, can we see our way to world salvation except through military means? And how can we get these military means except by penetrating the army as it exists?"

You mean by that, do you not, that you want your members, when inducted into the army service, to preach your doctrines to other soldiers in the army, and thereby defend them against military exploitation by their commanding officers? Isn't that a fair statement of what that means?

A: Our party is in favor of defending the rights of the rank and file soldiers, their democratic rights to decent treatment, their rights to express their opinions and to petition Congress, to elect their officers, at least their lower officers, generally protecting them against capitalist mistreatment.

Q: And that is what you want your members that are in the army now to do, to speak in favor of and to propagate those ideas?

A: Yes.

Q: In the army?

A: In the same way that they do it in the shop.

Q: But you do not think that would obstruct the military effort of the army?

A: If you will read that again you will see that we do not want any putsches. We say to the members "Do not make any putsches, and do not obstruct the army." It is our direct instruction to our people not to create obstruction of the military operation, but to confine their efforts to propagandistic work, to gain the sympathy and support of the rank and file masses.

Q: And you believe that your people can propagate that kind of stuff in the army and not obstruct the military efforts?

A: Yes, I think so. I think military life, as a matter of fact, will be a whole lot better, the more the rights and feelings of the rank and file soldiers are considered. The whole conception of militarism based on a rank and file without organization rights, and with arbitrary discipline imposed from above, without any expression of opinion or consideration for the feelings of the masses—we are just as much against that in the army as in the factory or in civil life.

Q: And the way you are talking now is the way you want your members to talk in the army, is it?

A: Each in his own way.

Q: Now, on June 29, 1940, the *Socialist Appeal* published this from the report of the *Manifesto of the Fourth International:* "Independently of the course of the war, we fulfill our basic task: We explain to the workers the irreconcilability between their interests and the interest of blood-thirsty capitalism; we mobilize the toilers against imperialism; we propagate the unity of the workers in all warring and neutral countries; we call for the fraternization of workers and soldiers within each country, and of soldiers with soldiers on the opposite side of the battlefront; we mobilize the women and youth against the war; we carry on constant, persistent, tireless preparation of the revolution—in the factories, in the mills, in the villages, in the barracks, at the front and in the fleet." You want the soldiers to do that, don't you?

A: Yes, I think that is a summation of the idea, for the soldiers and everybody to do that. That is the way to put an end to this slaughter.

Q: And you do not think that promulgating those ideas in the army during the war would obstruct the military efforts?

A: Not in the sense of opening up the front for the advantage of opposing armies, no. We are offering this solution to the soldiers of all the imperialist armies, but it does not mean and could not mean in any sense that we want to sabotage the operation of the American army in the interests of an opposing army. You will not find it there, or anywhere else in our literature.

Q: Well, that is a difference in points of view. In the *Socialist Appeal* of March 30, 1940, appears this editor's note in the Workers Forum, which says: "Entering the army upon being drafted is necessary for our work." What do you mean by that?

A: Is there a connecting sentence with it?

Q: It is from Exhibit 215-A. Mr. Smith will get that for us.

While Mr. Smith is looking for that, I will ask you about this from the *Socialist Appeal* of June 29, 1940, an article entitled "Enlistment Lag Forces Compulsion": "Meanwhile, let the workers remember this. When they are conscripted, let them not waste the period they spend in the army. They must learn everything there is to be learned about military training so that when the time comes they can use that training for the interests of the labor movement." What do you mean by that?

A: Meaning that the better trained the workers are, the better instructed in tactics and in military acts, the better they will be able to defend their socialist regime against the efforts of the minority reactionaries to overthrow it.

Q: This is the context from the Workers Forum, editor's note, March 30, 1940: "We follow Lenin; we oppose war, not as a measure of self-expression, but as an integral part of our struggle for the overthrow of capitalism. Entering the army upon being drafted is necessary for our work."

A: For our people, or people under our influence, to refuse to accept conscription, the only thing they would accomplish would be to simply isolate themselves from the generation who are going to decide things in the future, and such individual or minority actions are utterly false and incompatible with the aims of a party that can only realize its program by support of the majority.

That is why we oppose conscientious objectors, and why we oppose draft-evaders. We oppose all people who try to set themselves up as individuals against the majority. Our policy is to submit to the decision of the majority, but to oppose it in our political activities, to speak against it.

Q: In October 1938, you made a speech on "Ten Years of the Fight to Build a Revolutionary Party in the United States" in which you said this: "In the great Minneapolis strikes 'Trotskyism' revealed itself in the most dramatic fashion, as no bookman's dogma but a guide to the most militant and most effective action." What did you mean by that?

A: That in the strike in Minneapolis in 1934 some comrades affiliated with our party played a leading influence, or a part of the leading influence, and demonstrated in practice that the principles of Trotskyism are the best and most effective principles, and can be applied most effectively in the interests of the workers.

Q: Would this be a demonstration of this principle? In the *Militant* of July 12, 1941, under the heading, "Local 544-CIO's Proud and Stainless Record" this was said: "During the first drivers' strike of May 1934, the employers threw against the embattled transport workers the entire police force of Minneapolis and 5,000 special deputies armed with clubs and guns. In a historic battle—the 'Battle of Bulls Run'—the drivers fought the police and deputies to a standstill and chased them off the streets of the city." Is that Trotskyism demonstrating itself?

A: Well, I can give you my own opinion, that I am mighty proud of the fact that Trotskyism had some part in influencing the workers to protect themselves against that sort of violence.

Q: Well, what kind of violence do you mean?

A: This was what the deputies were organized for, to drive the workers off the street. They got a dose of their own medicine. I think the workers have a right to defend themselves. If that is treason, you can make the most of it.

Q: When you were tracing the history of the Russian Revolution, you said this: "The Kerensky government was losing ground because it was not solving any problems of the people. The Bolsheviks' slogans of "Bread" and other slogans—those were the slogans that the masses wanted. The Bolsheviks got a majority in the Petrograd Soviet. On November 7 was held the Congress of the All-Russian Soviets. The Bolsheviks had a majority there, and simultaneously with the meeting of the All-Russian Soviet, where the Bolsheviks had a majority, they took the power from the government." Now, do you want us to understand from that, that the Bolsheviks took power by virtue of a majority vote of the Congress of the Soviets?

A: That is right.

Q: Do you not mean that the contrary was true?

A: No, I do not.

Q: Don't you know that there was a planned insurrection

before the Congress, and that the insurrection actually took place before the Congress met?

A: No. The Congress met the morning after the struggle had begun, and confirmed the new government.

Q: The fact is that the insurrection was started and was completed before the Congress ever met, isn't it?

A: No, the power was in the Congress, and the Congress was the real power.

Q: Well, just answer my question, please. Isn't it a fact that the insurrection had been planned and actually carried out before the Congress ever met?

A: No. The question was submitted to the All-Russian Congress of the Soviets on November 7. That is why they call it the November 7 Revolution.

Q: Don't you know, further, that Lenin persistently warned against waiting for the Congress and doing it in a legal way?

A: Oh, that was one time that Lenin was overruled.

Q: And who won?

A: Trotsky won.

Q: Isn't it also a fact that Trotsky ridiculed the notion that it was done legally?

A: No, on the contrary, Trotsky commented on the legal sanction of the action by the Soviets. That was why it was delayed to November 7.

Q: Isn't it also true that he lulled Kerensky into inaction by pretending to wait until the Congress met so that it could be decided legally who was to take power?

A: He did not pretend to wait. He waited.

Q: I submit that the contrary is true, in that Mr. Trotsky said so, and I would like to read to you about ten pages or so from the *Lessons of October,* and then you can tell me whether I am right or wrong.

(Mr. Schweinhaut reads from pages 74 and 80 of Trotsky's *Lessons of October*.)

MR. GOLDMAN: I submit, Your Honor, that this book was ruled out of evidence. I have no objection if he wants to read one or two or perhaps three sentences, but to take advantage of cross-examination and put into evidence what the Court has ruled out, I think is going a little too far.

THE COURT: Well, this has to do, I suppose, with the dispute between counsel and witness, as to the facts with reference to which the witness takes one position and counsel takes another. Now this is an attempt to impeach the statements of the witness by the means indicated. I assume he has a right to do that. He may continue to read it.

MR. GOLDMAN: Exception.

(Mr. Schweinhaut reads pages 80–91 from Trotsky's *Lessons of October*.)

MR. SCHWEINHAUT: Now, am I right or wrong, Mr. Cannon, that the insurrection actually started and was concluded before the Soviet Congress put its seal of legality on it?

A: If you will permit me, I will show you where you are wrong. You misunderstood the whole thing; my authority for the evidence I gave here was Trotsky. He wrote the most authoritative and authentic history of the revolution. Perhaps I should mention several things to show where you are wrong:

First, those pages you have read show that there were three different opinions in the Central Committee of the Communist Party. Lenin said they had a majority, and they should take the power without waiting. There was the opinion of Zinoviev and Kamenev who thought the Bolsheviks did not have a majority and should not take the power. And the third opinion was Trotsky's that they could base the assumption of power on the legality of the Soviets.

Second, those pages you read prove that both the Mensheviks and the Bolsheviks derived their authority from the Soviets. In November it became clear that the Bolsheviks had won the majority in the Soviets. Kerensky, who formerly had the majority in the Soviets, prepared to move troops from the capital. What did the troops do? The troops refused to go until ordered by the Congress of Soviets. The Congress of the Soviets convened on November 7. It was revealed that the Bolsheviks had the majority, and their assumption of power was confirmed.

In this All-Russian Congress of Soviets were present the other parties who had been the majority of yesterday. They spoke and debated there. When the vote was taken, the Bolsheviks had the majority. The Bolsheviks offered to give proportionate places in the government to the other parties. They refused and walked off. The Bolsheviks did, as a matter of fact, incorporate into the government, a section of Kerensky's party, the left wing of the Social Revolutionary Party.

It seems to me that here is an excellent illustration of how a revolutionary party, after long propagandistic work, succeeded in a political crisis in winning over to its side a majority of the population represented in the most authoritative body, the Soviets of Workers', Soldiers' and Peasants' Deputies. And the Bolsheviks, adapting themselves to the legality of this authoritative body—

Q: Now, just a minute. Are you still telling us how it occurred, or are you just telling us now that you think it was a mighty fine thing?

A: No, I am explaining the legality of the development, as against your interpretation that it was illegal. And it seems to me—

Q: I don't want your opinion on that. If you want to go on and tell us what happened, all right. Don't characterize it.

A: I don't think you will ever get a more legal revolution than that.

MR. SCHWEINHAUT: That is all.

APPENDIX

A debate

Defense Policy *in the* Minneapolis Trial

A CRITICISM BY GRANDIZO MUNIS
AN ANSWER BY JAMES P. CANNON

A Criticism by Grandizo Munis

The initiation on the part of the United States government of a prosecution of the Socialist Workers Party and of the leaders of the Drivers Union of Minneapolis made us fear a decapitation, even though temporary, of our American movement. It filled us with a joyful hope at the same time, sure that the persecution by the bourgeois tribunals would popularize our revolutionary ideas when it gave our militants the opportunity to expound them completely and valiantly. It has been the norm and pride of the world revolutionary movement since the ringing reply of Louise Michel to her judges and of Karl Marx to the Bismarckian tribunal, to convert the accused into accusers and to employ the witness stand as a fortress from which to attack the reactionary powers. This attitude has been one of the principal forces of attraction of the revolutionary movement.

I experienced the first uneasiness that these results would be wasted totally or partially on reading the first published statement (the *Militant,* vol. V, no. 29) that seems to have set the tone for all the following statements. I recovered hope during the first sessions of the trial, during which our comrades energetically brought out the reactionary role of the government aided by Tobin against the Drivers of 544-CIO. But I again considered as lost a goodly part of the political benefits of the trial on reading the fundamental speeches and questionings of Comrade Cannon by Comrade Goldman, and by the prosecutor (Schweinhaut). It was there, replying to the political accusations—struggle against the war, advocacy of violence, overthrow of the government by force—where it was necessary to have raised the tone and turn the tables, accuse the government and the bourgeoisie of a reactionary conspiracy; of permanent violence against the majority of the population, physical, economic, moral, educative violence; of launching the population into a slaughter also by means of violence in order to defend the Sixty Families. On the contrary, it is on arriving at this part that the trial visibly weakens, our comrades shrink themselves, minimize the revolutionary significance of their ideas, try to make an honorable impression on the jury without taking into consideration that they should talk for the masses. For moments they border on a renunciation of principles. A few good words by Goldman in his closing speech cannot negate the lamentable, negative impression of his first speech and of the interrogation of Cannon.

I shall begin to criticize them by citing their words, taken textually from numbers 45, 47, 48, 50, 52, volume V, of the *Militant*.

Goldman in his opening statement to the jury:

"I repeat: *The objective and the aim of the party was to win through education and through propaganda a majority of the people of the United States*" (emphasis in the original).

It is exactly the same as the statement in July before the beginning of the trial. Answering a criticism made then from Mexico, a comrade of certain responsibility in the SWP replied that there was no need to worry because no one was in agreement with that statement. If no one was in agreement, then it was necessary to formulate another, that is evident, unless we have one policy for the masses and another for appearances before a bourgeois judge. It is hardly necessary to indicate the error of such a statement. It is understood by all, beginning by the one who made the statement, that our objective can in no way be only propaganda, nor will we win the majority by means of it. We are a party of propaganda in the sense that our numerical proportion prevents us or limits us to a minimum of action. But we are a party of revolutionary action—economic, political and educative—in essence and potentially, because our propaganda itself can tend only to action and only through action will we conquer the majority of the exploited and educate them for the taking of power.

I insist on these commonplaces because the euphemistic, sweetened character of this preliminary statement of Goldman, designed to reconcile the jury, is a compromise that has forced later statements much more grave. We will see further on.

Let us take the main problems and see how they have been dealt with in the trial.

Goldman begins with the following statement:

"We shall show that the Socialist Workers Party opposes sabotage. We shall show that Mr. Anderson's claim is absolutely wrong and based on no foundation whatever to the effect that we prefer the enemy, the imperialistic enemy of the United States, to defeat our government. It is absolutely false. What we want, as the evidence will show, is to have the workers and farmers establish their own government, and then to continue a real war against fascism."

Cannon even goes a bit further, replying to a question by Goldman: "A decision has been made, and is accepted by a majority of the people, to go to war. Our comrades have to comply with that."

And then Goldman asks: "You would not support the war?"

Cannon: "That is what I mean, we would not support the war, in a political sense."

And he even returns again to the point:

"We consider Hitler and Hitlerism the greatest enemy of mankind. We want to wipe it off the face of the earth. The reason we do not support a declaration of war by American arms is because we do not believe the American capitalists can defeat Hitler and fascism. We think Hitlerism can be destroyed only by way of conducting a war under the leadership of the workers."

In the first place, the decision to go to war has *not* "been made and accepted by a majority of the people." This statement can be criticized very strongly, a statement that we would censure very energetically if it were made by a centrist. In place of accusing the government of leading the American people to the slaughter against the will of the majority, instead of accusing it emphatically before the masses and of demonstrating to them how the parliamentarian majority acts against the majority of the people, Cannon endorses Roosevelt's decision as if it really corresponded to the majority of the people.

Yes, we submit to the war and our militants go to war, but not because it is a decision of the majority, but rather because it is imposed upon us by the violence of the bourgeois society just as wage exploitation is imposed. As in the factory, we should take advantage of all the opportunities to fight against the war and against the system that produces it, just as we fight against the boss in a factory, as a function of the general struggle against the capitalist system.

"We would not support the war in a political sense," says Cannon. Do we support it, perhaps, in some other sense? Social, economic? I do not see other senses. Does he perhaps mean by "to support" to accept the accomplished fact and to go to war? That is, to submit oneself, as we submit to the conditions imposed by a boss after the failure of a strike, but preparing ourselves for another. Why, then, equivocate so dangerously? I see no other reason but that our comrades have committed the very grave error of talking for a petty-bourgeois jury for the more immediate present, not foreseeing the future struggles. Would it not have been better to state: "We submit to your war, American bourgeois, because the violence of your society imposes it on us, the material violence of your arms. But the masses will turn against you. From today on, our party is with the masses in an irreconcilable struggle against your regime of oppression, misery and butchery. Therefore we will fight against your war with all means."

The equivocation and inexactness are permanent. It seems that we are platonic opponents of the war and that we limit ourselves to statements and propaganda, written or verbal, without action of any kind. To say that "we do not support a declaration of war because we do not believe the American capitalists can defeat Hitler and fascism" is to give the understanding that we would support it if we believed in that defeat; this induces those who believe in the victory of the United States to support it. Our rejection of the war is based on the character of the social regime that produces it, not on this or that belief about the defeat of fascism.

Immediately comes another equivocation: "We think Hitlerism can be destroyed, etc." Uniting that to the reiterated statements to the effect that we will not agitate among the soldiers, that we are a "political opposition" to the war, and to the, until now, limping exposition of military training under union control, can induce one to believe that we will be for the war *when* the control has been given to the unions. I believe it is necessary to clarify this, without leaving room for equivocation and I pronounce myself, for my part, against the war, even if control of the military service is achieved by the unions.

Immediately, Cannon undertakes to give a program for defeating Hitler by means of a workers' and farmers' government. I don't have to add a single comma, except that the entire questioning of Cannon closes with a double door, the road to establishing the workers' and farmers' government:

"Goldman: Now, until such time as the workers and farmers in the United States establish their own government and use their own methods to defeat Hitler, the Socialist Workers Party must submit to the majority of the people—is that right?

"Cannon: That is all we can do. That is all we propose to do."

All of which is the equivalent of folding one's arms after some lectures about the marvels of the workers' and farmers' government, in the hope that this will be formed by itself, or by God knows what sleight of hand.

This does not deal merely with an omission, but with a statement of passivity in the face of the imperialist war; something which at best is a bad education for the workers who have become interested in the trial and does not grant us any credit for tomorrow when the masses begin to act against the war.

Forced by statements of this sort—decidedly opportunist, I do not hesitate to say—Cannon sees himself obliged to ask for the expulsion from the party of the militants who organize protests in the army. He is carried to the incredible, to reject Lenin, Trotsky and Cannon himself.

Mr. Schweinhaut reads Cannon a paragraph of Lenin's from *The Revolution of 1905:*

> "'It is our duty in time of an uprising to exterminate ruthlessly all the chiefs of the civil and military authorities.' . . . You disagree with that?
>
> "Cannon: Yes, I don't know that that is in any way a statement of our party policy. . . . We do not agree with the extermination of anybody unless it is in case of an actual armed struggle, when the rules of war apply."

But what is "an uprising" except an armed struggle? Lenin also does not say "anybody" but rather the civil and military chiefs. Then why reject the paragraph?

Citing Cannon himself, Schweinhaut reads:

> "'The second point (struggle in the army) is to be careful, cautious. Make no putsches, make no premature moves that expose us and separate us from the masses. Go with the masses. . . . And how can we get these military means except by penetrating the army as it exists?' . . .
>
> "Schweinhaut: But you do not think that would obstruct the military effort of the army?
>
> "Cannon: If you will read that again you will see that we do not want any putsches. We say to the members: 'Do not make any putsches, and do not obstruct the army.' It is our direct instruction to our people not to create obstruction of the military operations, but to confine their efforts to propaganda."

I am wholeheartedly behind Cannon in his speech; but I categorically condemn Cannon before the jury, deforming himself, minimizing, reducing to words the revolutionary action of the party. And I will be equally behind and I propose that the party be behind the militants and soldiers who carry out acts of protests in the army, remembering that they do not deal with "putsches, premature movements." Revolutionary action in time of war is absolutely impossible without obstructing in a greater or lesser degree the military activities. Therefore, the principle of revolutionary defeatism, which the American party and the International have and cannot renounce. Contrary to what Goldman gave to understand in the first quotation, we are for the intensification of the class struggle, in the rearguard and in the army, including, if this can, provoking the defeat of our bourgeoisie: "From the point of view of a revolution in their own country, the defeat of their own imperialist government is undoubtedly the better evil" (Trotsky, June 1940). It is worse in advice to the workers to disauthorize agitation and protests in the army, only to speak against it. I believe that our comrades have lost a good opportunity to make the workers understand why they should act always by means of the word and by means of collective actions. The questioning of Cannon presented a completely false perspective to the workers, of comfortable propaganda, where it deals with a terrible struggle by all means from small protests to insurrections by groups, from partial fraternizations to wiping out the fronts. But, from an error of perspective, one passes to an error of fact; therefore the defendants saw themselves forced to condemn sabotage in general, as though it dealt with something criminal. I believe that sabotage is a method for tactical use whose application at certain moments can be productive of contrary effects to what is intended but which is absolutely indispensable in the critical moments of struggle.

An example will demonstrate it. Suppose that in a certain part of the front conditions of fraternization are produced. Fraternization will never be produced simultaneously on both sides of a large front nor in the same proportion. Immediately the military chiefs will give orders to mobilize, attack or reinforce the fronts with soldiers less disposed to embrace the "enemy." Is it not our duty then to sabotage in the greatest degree the renewal of combat, to give time to the fraternization, to impede the command from dominating the situation? Sabotage will be the only means at hand for the soldiers to extend and precipitate the fraternization, until the fail of *the two* fronts. Nevertheless, there exists the danger that the enemy command may dominate its front and taking advantage of the disorganization, undertake a victorious offensive. There is no way out for an effective fraternization if one wishes to avoid that "danger."

Sabotage and defeatism will unite at a certain moment as the two main elements in the reactions of the masses against the imperialist war. The party should not and cannot renounce defeatism without condemning itself to a perpetual sterile chat against the war.

What seems even more lamentable to me is that one can intuit from the trial that it is not only a question of something said especially for the jury. For moments there is evidence that the defendants really consider sabotage a crime. If I am not mistaken—and I hope I am—this is a dangerous moral predisposition. Sabotage will be the reaction of the masses against the imperialist war. Why be ashamed of it? Why be ashamed that the masses react, as they can, against the monstrous crime of the present war? It would have been easy to defend it as a principle and throw the responsibility on the leaders of the present war. Can we condemn the future sabotage of the masses when the war is a gigantic sabotage of the bourgeoisie against the masses, against civilization and humanity? Instead of receiving this idea, the workers who heard our comrades will have left, burdened with a prejudice against sabotage.

Says Goldman:

> "The evidence will further show as Mr. Anderson himself indicated, that we prefer a peaceful transition to socialism; but that we analyze all the conditions in society, we analyze history, and on the basis of this analysis we predict, *we predict,* that after the majority of the people in the United States will want socialism established, that the minority, organized by the financiers and by capitalists, will use violence to prevent the establishment of socialism. That is what we predict."

Why not ask forgiveness, besides, for seeing ourselves painfully obliged to employ violence against the bourgeoisie? Even neutralizing oneself to a mere diviner, the prediction is completely false. It is not necessary to poke into the future to discover the violence of the reactionary minority throughout society. The accusation lends itself ideally to launching a thorough attack against capitalist society and to show the American workers that the so-called American democracy is no more than a dictatorship of the bourgeoisie. Among the workers who have read or listened to Cannon and Goldman, there must be many who have experienced the daily violence of bourgeois society, during strikes, demonstrations, meetings; all of them without exception experience the normal violence of either working for a wage established in the labor market or of perishing; a violence much more lamentable is the imposition of the war; educative violence; informative violence imposed by the newspaper trusts. Far from receiving a notion of the environment in which they live and far from preparing their spirit for rebellion against this environment, the workers watching the trial have been pacified in respect to the present. Only in the future will the bourgeoisie employ violence.

Besides, it is completely inexact and contributes toward putting the workers to sleep, to tell them that the bourgeoisie will employ violence "after the majority of the people in the United States will want socialism established." It uses violence already, always employs it, the bourgeoisie knows of no other method of government but violence. The workers and farmers should respond to the daily violence of the bourgeoisie with majority and organized violence of the poor masses. We do not predict, but rather we assure, we ask, we advocate temporary violence of the majority against the permanent organic violence of the reactionary minority. It is necessary to break the democratic prejudices of the American proletariat; but statements like that rock them to sleep.

"After all," an inexpert worker may say, "what certainty can one have that the bourgeoisie will employ violence. These men who know a lot only predict it; then for the moment, I need not organize to counter the violence of the reactionaries." This tendency to inaction will be accentuated if the worker in question continues reading: "We expect to prove that the defendants never advocated, never incited, to violence, but simply predicted the violence of the reactionary minority." It is clear when they do not do that, it is not yet necessary.

And once more, as we saw in the case of the war, all possibility of inciting to action is closed by the preliminary obstruction. Following their sense, the perspective presented by our comrades for the coming years is also false.

What means will be valuable to us for conquering the majority of the proletariat and poor farmers? (Not merely the people as is repeated constantly in the examination. The petty bourgeoisie can be neutralized without being won over.)

I do not find in the long pages of the interrogation of Cannon anything other than propaganda, propaganda and more propaganda, as if it dealt with recommending a patent medicine for baldness. A brief paragraph, uttered in a good direction by Cannon, is not, unfortunately, sufficiently explicit and energetic: "Of course, we don't limit ourself simply to that prediction. We go further, and advise the workers to bear this in mind and prepare themselves not to permit the reactionary outlived minority to frustrate the will of the majority."

Then, why not raise the voice at this point and call upon the workers to organize their own violence against the reactionary violence? Immediately afterward, the perspective of struggle against the fascist bands is perfectly sketched by Cannon; but one notes that it deals with a nonexistent perspective in an immediate form as if today against the false democracy it were unnecessary to organize the shock forces of the proletariat. It is something that is not clearly stated, it lends itself to equivocation and is reinforced by the final insistence in denying the existence (today) of any workers' guard. At any rate, the line that our comrades have followed in not taking advantage of the trial to indicate to the masses how and why they should exercise their own violence is incorrect. Instead we have the lamentable dialogue between Cannon and Goldman destined to pacify the easily frightened conscience of the jury about who initiates the violence.

In one manner or another it is supposed that we are going to conquer the majority for socialism. Then:

"Goldman: What is meant by the expression 'overthrow of the capitalist state'?

"Cannon: That means to replace it by a workers' and farmers' government; that is what we mean.

"Goldman: What is meant by the expression 'destroy the machinery of the capitalist state'?

"Cannon: By that we mean that *when* (my emphasis) we set up the workers' and farmers' government in this country, the functioning of this government, its tasks, its whole nature, will be so profoundly and radically different from the functions, tasks and nature of the bourgeois state, that we will have to replace it all along the line."

All the revolutionary, violent process, the *civil war* that must precede the establishment of the workers' and farmers' government and the proletarian state, is palmed away; I cannot find another word more euphemistic. Therefore, when a little bit later Cannon has to circumscribe himself, he gives a definition of the soviet, such as an abbreviated encyclopedia would give, hushing everything that deals with its function as an organism of struggle, in competition and opposition to the organisms of the bourgeois power.

What other thing can the workers' and farmers' government be than the culmination of the struggle of the proletariat and farmers against the bourgeoisie? That struggle has to be pushed from now on, and beginning with the opening of the revolutionary crisis, it will develop "in crescendo," to the point at which the masses will create soviets or councils that direct the general struggle of the proletariat against the bourgeoisie, foresee the necessities of that struggle, including arms, and permit within its fold a liberty of ideological struggle so that the masses can elect those who best represent them. Only then, when the revolutionary tendency has acquired a majority of the soviets—not in the parliamentarian elections—the violent seizure of power will destroy the bourgeois state, leaving the soviets as the base of the proletarian state.

Cannon stated that the machine of the bourgeois state will be destroyed "when we set up the workers' and farmers' government." But the possibility of such a government does not open until *after* we have destroyed that machine. Cannon knows this perfectly, and undoubtedly, proposes to act accordingly. But in that case, I insist, why lose the excellent and rare opportunity to give the workers a lesson, indicating to them without subterfuge the road to the struggle and power, accusing at the same time the bourgeoisie of a reactionary and profascist course? The predictions about how the social dialectic is going to reinforce our positions do not have any real value for the workers. The revolutionary process is seen here as the schoolbooks will describe it in five hundred years. The workers today need an indication of the dynamics of the class struggle, the forms of organization, methods of struggle up to the civil war, slogans, and included there is a need for proud valor against the class enemy, something which has been rare in the trial. The general tone has been not to accuse but to apologize to a point that makes one feel embarrassed at times; not to indicate and propose actions and immediate means for the struggle against the bourgeoisie and against the war, but rather to dilute our ideas into humanitarianism and to veil their *active* value with predictions of knowledge as if it were not honorable to employ violence against the present corrupted bourgeois democracy.

Something completely demonstrative of the foregoing is that our comrades have cited as witnesses in their defense—Jefferson, Lincoln, the Bible, Lloyd George, MacDonald; but when Marx, Lenin, Trotsky and even Cannon appear, they are rejected as nonofficial mouthpieces of our organization. This attitude, not very valiant, cannot conquer much sympathy, or at least cannot conquer as much as the opposite attitude would conquer.

I know perfectly well that I am not teaching anything to anybody. What I have said is known better by the comrades to whom it refers. They will agree with me in relation to the principles referred to, except perhaps, in the problems of military training under trade-union control, and sabotage—questions that it is urgent to clarify in the party and in the International. I find no more reason for their attitude in the trial than considerations that it would be a "useful maneuver." But it is precisely that I consider it a very grave error to substitute maneuvers for principles in moments so important for the political future of the party. I believe and propose as a general principle that in similar trials our responsible militants accept all responsibility for the practical action of our ideas. This is worth more than a light sentence at the price of a pretty and deceptive polish. I propose that this criticism be published in the internal bulletins of the International and of the Socialist Workers Party.

January 7, 1942

Note: This criticism has been written with extreme rush, in order not to lose an immediate opportunity to transmit it. I have not taken more than the paragraphs that first struck my eyes. Therefore, I reserve the possibility of amplifying it.

An Answer by James P. Cannon

In the Minneapolis "sedition" trial, as in the months-long trade-union battle which preceded and led up to it, the American Trotskyists were put to the test and compelled to show what stuff they are made of. In both instances they conducted themselves in a manner befitting disciples of Trotsky and met the test in all respects.

In the fight with the trade-union bureaucracy, which attracted national attention, it was clearly shown who the real leaders of militant labor, the real men of principle, really are. In the trial before the bourgeois court the party, by the conduct of all its members involved, earned the right to the confidence of the revolutionary workers. The two struggles, which in reality were two sides of one and the same struggle, marked a climactic point in the activity of the American movement which had developed in a restricted circle since its inception thirteen years before.

During that time the party, with some local exceptions, had gained the attention only of the vanguard of class-conscious workers. At the trial we had the opportunity, for the first time, to speak to the masses—to the people of the United States. We seized upon the opportunity and made the most of it, and applied in practice without a serious fault the basic principles which had been assimilated in a long preparatory period. Since then the movement in the United States stands on higher ground.

A critical study and discussion of the trial cannot fail to be of the highest value to the Fourth International, especially to those sections which have yet to reach the turn in the road which leads from the propaganda circle to mass work. For our part, we welcome the discussion and will do our best to contribute something useful to it.

From the first moment after the indictment was brought against us in the Federal Court at Minneapolis last July we recognized that the attack had two aspects, and we appraised each of them, we think, at their true significance. The prosecution was designed to outlaw the party and deprive it, perhaps for a long time, of the active services of a number of its most experienced leaders. At the same time it was obvious that the mass trial, properly handled on our part, could give us our first real opportunity to make the party and its principles known to wide circles of workers and to gain a sympathetic hearing from them.

Our strategy, from the beginning, took both sides of the problem into account. Naturally, we decided to utilize to the fullest extent each and every legal protection, technicality and resource available to us under the law and the Constitution. A party leadership hesitating or neglecting to do this would frivolously jeopardize the legality of the party and show a very wasteful attitude indeed toward party cadres. Such a leadership would deserve only to be driven out with sticks and stones.

On the other hand, we planned to conduct our defense in court not as a "criminal" defense but as a propaganda offensive. Without foolishly disregarding or provoking the jury or needlessly helping the prosecutor, it was our aim to use the courtroom as a forum to popularize the principles of our movement. We saw in this second proposition our main duty and opportunity and never for a moment intended to let purely legalistic considerations take precedence over it. Therefore we sternly rejected the repeated advice of attorneys—some who assisted Goldman in the trial of the case as well as others who were consulted about participation—to eliminate or play down our "propaganda" program and leave the defense policy to the lawyers.

From the rather unhappy experiences of past trials of militants in the courts of the United States we knew what following such advice would mean: Deny or keep quiet about the revolutionary principles of the movement; permit the lawyers to disavow and ridicule the defendants, and pass them off as somewhat foolish people belonging to a party which is not to be taken seriously; and depend on spread-eagle speeches of the lawyers to the jury to get the defendants off some way or other.

The October plenum-conference of the party unanimously endorsed the National Committee's recommendations on court-room policy. The resolution of the conference laid down the policy as follows:

"The policy of the party in defending itself in court, obligatory for all party members under indictment, can only be one that is worthy of our movement and our tradition; no attempt to water down or evade our revolutionary doctrine, but, on the contrary, to defend it militantly. At the same time we maintain that we have a legal right under the Bill of Rights to propagate our principles."

That is the policy we took with us to the trial. It guided us at every step in the proceedings. And we think it can be safely said that the policy has been amply vindicated by the results. Our principles were widely popularized, a hundred or a thousand times better than ever before, and our conduct before the court has met with approval and sympathy from the militant workers who followed the trial and read the testimony.

The trial was by far our greatest propaganda success. Moreover, even those workers who disagree with our program, have approved and applauded our conduct in court as worthy of people who take their principles seriously. Such is the testimony of all comrades who have reported on the reaction of the workers to the trial. On a recent tour across the country from branch to branch of the party we heard the same unvarying report everywhere.

Naturally, our work in the trial was not perfect; we did only the best we could within the narrow limits prescribed by the court. More qualified people can quite easily point out things here and there which might have been done more cleverly. We can readily acknowledge the justice of such criticisms without thereby admitting any guilt on our part, for socialism does not require that all be endowed with equal talent, but only that each give according to his ability. It is a different matter when Comrade Munis—and other critics of our policy—accuse us of misunderstanding our task and departing from Marxist principles in the trial. To them we are obliged to say firmly: No, the misunderstanding is all on your side. The correct understanding of our task in the courtroom and the sanction of the Marxist authorities, are on our side.

In undertaking to prove this contention we must begin with a brief analysis of a point overlooked by Munis as well as by the others: the social environment in which the trial was conducted. Our critics nowhere, by so much as a single word, refer to the objective situation in the United States; the political forms still prevailing here; the degree of political maturity— more properly, immaturity—of the American proletariat; the relation of class forces; the size and status of the party—in short, to the specific peculiarities of our problem which should determine our method of approach to workers hearing us for the first time from the sounding board of the trial.

Our critics talk in terms of trials in general and principles in general, which, it would appear, are always to be formulated and explained to the workers in general in precisely the same way. We, on the contrary, dealt with a specific trial and attempted to explain ourselves to the workers as they are in the United States in the year 1941. Thus we clash with our critics at the very point of departure—the analysis, the method. Our answer to their criticism must take the same form.

We shall begin by first setting forth the concrete environmental circumstances in which our party functioned in the United States at the time of the trial and the specific tasks and propaganda techniques which, in our opinion, were thereby imposed. Then we shall proceed to submit our position, as well as that of our critics, to the criterion which must be decisive for all of us: the expressions of the Marxist teachers on the application of the points of principle under discussion.[*]

The United States, where the trial took place, is by far the richest of all the capitalist nations, and because of that has been one of the few such nations still able to afford the luxury of bourgeois democratic forms in the epoch of the decline and

---

[*] All quotations cited in this document are from the English texts.

decay of capitalism. Trade unions, which have been destroyed in one European country after another in the past decade, have flourished and more than doubled their membership in the United States in the same period—partly with governmental encouragement. Free speech and free press, obliterated or reduced to travesty in other lands, have been virtually unrestricted here. Elections have been held under the normal bourgeois democratic forms, traditional in America for more than a century, and the great mass of the workers have freely participated in them. The riches and favored position of bourgeois America have also enabled it, despite the devastating crisis, to maintain living standards of the workers far above those of any other country.

These objective circumstances have unfailingly affected both the mentality of the workers and the fortunes of the revolutionary political movement. The revolutionary implications of the shaken economy, propped up for the time being by the armaments boom, are as yet but slightly reflected in the consciousness of the workers. In their outlook they are far from revolutionary. "Politics" to them means voting for one or another of the big capitalist parties. The simple fact that the organized labor movement has not yet resorted to independent political action, even on a reformist basis, but remains in its political activity an appendage of the Roosevelt political party—this simple fact in itself shows conclusively that the American workers have not yet begun to translate their fierce militancy in the field of economic strikes, directed at individual employers, into terms of independent politics directed against the employers as a class. As for the Marxist party, with its program of the revolutionary transformation of society, it has been able in such an environment to attract the attention of only a few thousands to its message and to recruit into its ranks a still smaller number of the most advanced and class-conscious militants.

The forty million American workers, casting an almost solid labor vote for Roosevelt, remain in the first primitive stages of class political development; they are soaked through and through with bourgeois democratic illusions; they are discontented to a certain extent and partly union-conscious but not class-conscious; they have a fetishistic respect for the federal government as the government of all the people and hope to better conditions for themselves by voting for "friendly" bourgeois politicians; they hate and fear fascism which they identify with Hitler; they understand socialism and communism only in the version disseminated by the bourgeois press and are either hostile or indifferent to it; the real meaning of socialism, the revolutionary Marxist meaning, is unknown to the great majority.

Such were the general external factors, and such was the mentality of the American workers, confronting our party at the time of the Minneapolis trial, October, November, and December 1941. What specific tasks, what propaganda techniques were imposed thereby? It seems to us that the answers are obvious. The task was to *get a hearing* for our ideas from the forum of the trial. These ideas had to be simplified as much as possible, *made plausible* to the workers and illustrated whenever possible by familiar examples from American history. We had to address ourselves to the workers not in general, not an abstraction, but as they exist in reality in the United States in the year 1941. We had to recognize that the forms of democracy and the legality of the party greatly facilitate this propaganda work and must not be lightly disregarded. It was not our duty to facilitate the work of the prosecuting attorney but to make it more difficult, insofar as this could be done without renouncing any principle. Such are the considerations which guided us in our work at the trial.

Our critics do not refer to them; evidently they did not even think of them. Our method is a far different method than the simple repetition of formulas about "action" which requires nothing but a good memory. More precisely, it is the Marxist method of applying principles to concrete circumstances in order to popularize a party and create a movement which can lead to action in the real life of the class struggle, not on the printed page where the "action" of sectarian formalists always begins and ends.

The accomplishment of our main task—to use the courtroom as a forum from which to speak to those American workers, as they are, who might hear us for the first time—required, in our judgment, not a call to arms but patient, schoolroom *explanations* of our doctrines and ourselves, and a quiet tone. Therefore we adapted, not our principles but our propaganda technique to the occasion as we understood it. The style of propaganda and the tone which we employed are not recommended as a universally applicable formula. Our propaganda style and tone were simply designed to serve the requirements, in the given situation, of a small minority Marxist party in a big country of democratic capitalism in the general historic circumstances above described.

Comrade Munis accuses us of popularizing our propaganda and defending ourselves (and the party's legality) at the expense of principle. Our statements at the trial are held to be "decidedly opportunist"; to "border on a renunciation of principles." Following such and similar assertions we are informed that "it is a very grave error to substitute maneuvers for principles." This maxim—not entirely original in our movement—can be accepted with these provisos: that the maxim be understood; that a distinction be made between "maneuvers" which serve principle and those which contradict it; and that it be applied to actual and not imaginary sacrifices of principle. This is the gist of the whole matter. The Marxist teachers did not change their principles, but in explaining them they frequently changed their manner and tone and points of emphasis to suit the occasion. We had a right and a duty to do the same. An examination of our testimony from this standpoint will bring different conclusions from those which our critics have so hastily drawn.

We were charged in the first count of the indictment with "conspiracy to overthrow the government by force and violence" in violation of the statute of 1861 which was originally directed against the slaveholders' rebellion. In the second count we were charged, among other things, with "conspiracy to *advocate* the overthrow of the government by force and violence" in violation of the Smith Act of 1940.

In our defense we flatly denied we had either "conspired" or "advocated" violence, and by that we did not in the least intend to deny or repudiate any principle of Marxism. We claimed the right to *explain* our position. We testified that we prefer a peaceful social transformation; that the bourgeoisie takes the initiative in violence and will not permit a peaceful change; that we advise the workers to bear this in mind and prepare to *defend themselves* against the violence of the outlived reactionary minority class.

This formula—which is 100 percent correct in the essence of the matter and unassailable from the standpoint of Marxist authority—did not coincide with the contentions of the prosecuting attorney, nor help him to prove his case against us. But that was not our duty. From entirely opposite considerations our exposition does not meet with the approval of Comrade Munis nor coincide with his conceptions. That is not our duty either, because his conceptions are arbitrary and formalistic—and therefore false.

The prosecutor wanted to limit the whole discussion of socialism to the single question of "force and violence." We on the other hand—for the first time in an American courtroom—tried to make an exposition, if only a brief and sketchy one, of the whole range of Marxist theory, as in an elementary study class for uninitiated workers, to the extent that this was possible within the narrow framework prescribed by the court's rules and the repeated objections of the prosecutor, assigning the question of force in the social revolution to its proper proportionate place and putting the responsibility for it where it properly belongs—on the shoulders of the outlived class.

We carried out this task to the best of our ability at the trial. Of course, thesis precision and full-rounded explanation are hardly possible in a rapid-fire impromptu dialogue, with answers compressed to extreme brevity by time limitations, prosecutor's objections and court rulings. We cannot claim such precision and amplitude for our answers, and reasonable people should not demand it of us. Even Trotsky admitted the possibility of flaws in testimony which he gave in somewhat similar but more favorable circumstances before the Dewey Commission. In reply to Ver, who had criticized one of his answers in the published record of the Inquiry, he said:

> "It is possible that there is some lack of precision in the stenographic report. It is not a matter here either of a programmatic text well thought out, or even of an article, but of a stenographic report drawn up by the Commission. You know that I did not even have the chance to revise it myself. Some misunderstandings, imprecisions may have crept in. Enemies can make use of them, but serious comrades must grasp the question in its totality" (*Internal Bulletin* of the Socialist Workers Party, No. 3).

Here it may be in order to explain that American court procedure, unlike that of many other countries, does not permit defendants to introduce worked-out statements and "declarations." They must answer orally, they must make their answers short and are liable to be cut off at any time by the objection of the prosecutor or the ruling of the judge. In such an atmosphere a witness is under constant pressure to condense his answers and to omit explanations which may be necessary for full clarity but which are not interesting to the court.

We mention these factors only to ask the same kind of reasonable allowance for shortcomings which Trotsky asked, not to disavow anything we said. By and large, making all due acknowledgement of imperfections, omissions and inadequacies in the oral testimony, we accomplished our propagandistic aims at the trial, and we stand on the record. The court record, published in thousands of copies, became and will remain our most effective propaganda document. It is an honest and forthright revolutionary record. Nobody will succeed in discrediting it.

What did we say about violence in the transformation of society from capitalism to socialism? This is what we said:

1) The Marxists prefer a peaceful transition. "The position of

the Marxists is that the most economical and preferable, the most desirable method of social transformation, by all means, is to have it done peacefully."

2) "It is the opinion of all Marxists that it will be accompanied by violence."

3) That opinion "is based, like all Marxist doctrine, on a study of history, the historical experiences of mankind in the numerous changes of society from one form to another, the revolutions which accompanied it, and the resistance which the outlived classes invariably put up against the new order. Their attempt to defend themselves against the new order, or to suppress by violence the movement for the new order, has resulted in every important social transformation up to now being accompanied by violence."

4) The ruling class always initiates the violence, "always the ruling class; always the outlived class that doesn't want to leave the stage when the time has come. They want to hang on to their privileges, to reinforce them by violent measures, against the rising majority *and they run up against the mass violence of the new class,* which history has ordained shall come to power."

5) That is our prediction. But "of course, we don't limit ourselves simply to that prediction. We go further, and advise the workers to bear this in mind and prepare themselves not to permit the reactionary outlived minority to frustrate the will of the majority."

"Q: What role does the rise and existence of fascism play with reference to the possibility of violence?

"A: Well, that is really the nub of the whole question, because the reactionary violence of the capitalist class, expressed through fascism, is invoked against the workers. Long before the revolutionary movement of the workers gains the majority, fascist gangs are organized and subsidized by millions in funds from the biggest industrialists and financiers, as the example of Germany showed—and these fascist gangs undertake to break up the labor movement by force, raid the halls, assassinate the leaders, break up the meetings, burn the printing plants, and destroy the possibility of functioning long before the labor movement has taken the road of revolution.

"I say that is the nub of the whole question of violence. If the workers don't recognize that, and do not begin to defend themselves against the fascists, they will never be given the possibility of voting on the question of revolution. They will face the fate of the German and Italian proletariat and they will be in the chains of fascist slavery before they have a chance of any kind of a fair vote on whether they want socialism or not.

"It is a life and death question for the workers that they organize themselves to prevent fascism, the fascist gangs, from breaking up the workers' organizations, and not to wait until it is too late. That is the program of our party."

That is all any Marxist really needs to say on the question of violence in a capitalist court or at a propaganda meeting for workers at the present time in the United States. It tells the truth, conforms to principle, and protects the legal position of the party. The workers will understand it too. To quote Shakespeare's Mercutio: "'Tis not so deep as a well, nor so wide as a church-door; but 'tis enough, 'twill serve."

Comrade Munis, however, is not satisfied with our "lamentable dialogue," allegedly "destined to pacify the easily frightened conscience of the jury about who initiates the violence." The above-quoted answer advising the workers to "bear in mind" the violent course of the ruling class and "prepare themselves," is not "sufficiently explicit and energetic." (He underestimates the acuteness of the workers.) "Why not," says Comrade Munis, "raise the voice at this point and call upon the workers to organize their own violence against the reactionary violence?"

Why not? Because it was not necessary or advisable either to raise the voice or issue any call for action at this time. We were talking, in the first place, for the benefit of the uninitiated worker who would be reading the testimony in the paper or in pamphlet form. We needed a calm and careful exposition in order to get his attention. This worker is by no means waiting impatiently for our call to violent action. Quite the contrary, he ardently believes in the so-called democracy, and the first question he will ask, if he becomes interested in socialism, is: "Why can't we get it peacefully, by the ballot?" It is necessary to *patiently explain* to him that, while we would prefer it that way, the bosses will not permit it, will resort to violence against the majority, and that the workers must *defend* themselves and their *right* to change things. Our *defensive* formula is not only legally unassailable, "for the jury," as our critics contemptuously remark—as though twenty-eight indicted people in their right senses, and a party threatened with illegality, can afford the luxury of disregarding the jury. It is also the best formula for effective propaganda.

These defensive formulas are not our invention; they come directly from the great Marxists who did not believe in the good will of the class enemies and knew how to organize action, that is, mass action, against them. And these same teachers and organizers of mass actions likewise never failed to appreciate the value of democratic forms and party legality and to hang onto them and utilize them to the fullest extent possible. Our teachers did not shrink from force; they never deluded the workers with the promise of a peaceful, democratic transformation of society. But they didn't speak of violence always in the same way, in the same tone and with the same emphasis. Always, in circumstances in any way comparable to ours, they have spoken as we spoke at the trial. Proof of this is abundant and overwhelming.

The *first* formulated statement of the communist position on the question of violence and the transition to socialism appears in Engels' *Principles of Communism,* a "catechism" written in 1847 which is generally regarded as the first draft of the *Communist Manifesto.* Engels wrote:

"Question Sixteen: Will it be possible to bring about the abolition of private property by peaceful methods?

"Answer: It is a thing greatly to be desired, and communists would be the last persons in the world to stand in the way of a peaceful solution" (Marx and Engels, Collected Works, vol. 6, pp. 349–50).

Engels didn't promise such a solution and he didn't forget to add: "Should the oppressed proletariat at long last be goaded into a revolution, the communists will rally to the cause of the workers and be just as prompt to act as they are now to speak."

The *last* statement of Marxist authority, expressed by Trotsky ninety-three years later, follows the same pattern as that of Engels. In the summer of 1940 the Dies Committee conducted a raid on a comrade's house in Texas and carried off some party literature. Anticipating an attack on the legal position of the Socialist Workers Party, Comrade Trotsky wrote us a letter, advising us how to formulate our propaganda and defend ourselves "from the legal point of view" and warning us not "to furnish any pretext for persecutions." This letter, as though written to answer in advance the ultraradical quibbling about the Minneapolis trial, was printed in *Fourth International,* October 1940, p. 126. Trotsky wrote:

"The Texas story is very important. The attitude of the people involved can become decisive from the legal point of view.

"We, of course, cannot imitate the Stalinists who proclaim their absolute devotion to the bourgeois democracy. However, we do not wish to furnish any pretext for persecutions.

"In this case, as in any others, we should speak the truth as it is; namely, the best, the most economical and favorable method for the masses would be to achieve the transformation of this society by democratic means. The democracy is also necessary for the organization and education of the masses. That is why we are always ready to defend the democratic rights of the people by our own means. However, we know on the basis of tremendous historical experience that the 60 Families will never permit the democratic realization of socialist principles. At a given moment the 60 Families will inevitably overthrow, or try to overthrow, the democratic institutions and replace them by a reactionary dictatorship.

This is what happened in Italy, in Germany and in the last days in France—not to mention the lesser countries. We say in advance that we are ready to reject such an attempt with arms in hands, and crush the fascist dictatorship by a proletarian dictatorship.

"This position corresponds to the historical reality and is juridically unattackable."

These words, written by the founder of our movement in the last month of his life, were not chance remarks thrown off at random. They were written in direct connection with an expected prosecution, and he specifically warned us that "the attitude of the people involved can become decisive from the legal point of view." He knew the value of party legality and did not want us to jeopardize it needlessly. Do not, he said almost in so many words, accept the prosecuting attorney's accusation that we advocate conspiratorial violence by a minority. Present the question in a way which "corresponds to historical reality" and which is, at the same time, by its defensive formulation, "juridically unattackable."

That letter was the guiding line for our policy at the trial. We took the words of Trotsky as Marxist authority. For us there is no higher. Our movement, the movement of the Fourth International which stems directly from the struggle of the Trotskyist Opposition in Russia since 1923, embodies in its doctrine and its tradition the whole of Marxism and the whole of the precepts and example of Lenin, developed and applied to conditions of the post-Lenin period. We know it is the fashion in late years for some people to contrast Lenin to Trotsky and to refer to Lenin as the primary authority. The Oehlerites in the United States, for example, advertise themselves as "Leninists" of this type; and even Shachtman, dabbling with radicalism for a season, tried to invoke Lenin against the military policy elaborated by Trotsky. There is no more truth or merit in this burlesque than there was in the attempt of the opportunists during the First World War to appeal to Marx and Engels against Lenin.

All four of the great Marxist authorities—Marx, Engels, Lenin and Trotsky—are united in an uninterrupted continuity of experience reflected in Marxist thought. For us, Lenin is Marx in the epoch of the First World War and the October Revolution. Trotsky is Lenin in the epoch of Stalinist degeneration and the struggle against it, the epoch of fascism and the Second World War and the preparation of the new rise of the international revolution of the proletariat.

These "Leninists"—God save the mark!—are fond of repeating isolated quotations from Lenin as fixed and final answers to current problems which arise ever new and in infinite variations of circumstance. A greater distortion of Leninism—which is a method, not a collection of bible texts —can hardly be imagined. They repeat the words of Lenin on this or that occasion without understanding that Lenin did not always repeat himself and had nothing but contempt for such thought-saving substitutes for living Marxism. An instructive sample of this practice is the attempt of Munis to picture us as "rejecting" Lenin because we took the liberty of saying a sentence he wrote about insurrection in czarist Russia in 1906 is not applicable for our propaganda in the United States in 1941.

Our frank avowal before the court that we are disciples of Lenin is not enough to satisfy Munis. Our statement that in our movement "he holds a position of esteem on a level with Marx" that "the basic ideas and doctrines, practiced, promulgated and carried out by Lenin, are supported by our movement"—these declarations, in the judgment of our critic, are not sufficient to constitute an acceptance of Lenin. He seems to think it is necessary to repeat and accept as gospel every word Lenin said on every occasion regardless of what Lenin himself may have said on the same subject on other occasions.

He cites the question of Mr. Schweinhaut, the prosecutor, reading a sentence from Lenin's *The Revolution of 1905:* "'It is our duty in time of an uprising to exterminate ruthlessly all the chiefs of the civil and military authorities.' . . . You disagree with that?"

Naturally we denied that this is a statement of party policy here and now, modifying it as follows: "We do not agree with the extermination of anybody unless it is in case of an actual armed struggle, when the rules of war apply." In reality this was saying, out of deference to Lenin, a great deal more than needs to be said on the subject of extermination before a capitalist court or in a propaganda speech in the United States at the present time. But this does not satisfy Munis. Why, he demands, say "anybody" instead of "the civil and military chiefs"? "Why reject the paragraph?" We must repeat Lenin word for word!

Why must we? *Lenin didn't repeat himself word for word.* Far from it, he changed and modified such formulas to suit occasion without ceremony. In fact, on the very eve of the October Revolution, he changed this particular formula so radically as to give it a quite different, "milder" meaning in order better to serve his political aims at the time. In his letter to the Central Committee, dated September 26–27, 1917, *a letter calling for the organization of the insurrection,* he omits any reference to "extermination" and simply says: "We must arrest the general staff and the government" (Lenin, *Collected Works,* vol. 26, p. 27; our emphasis).

On still another occasion, September 14–16, 1917, offering a "compromise" to the Social Revolutionary and Menshevik majority, Lenin proposed that they form an SR-Menshevik government responsible only to the Soviets. Such a government, he said, "in all probability could secure a peaceful *forward* march of the whole Russian Revolution." Should the proposition be accepted by the SR's and Mensheviks, then:

"No other condition would, I think, be advanced by the Bolsheviks, who would be confident that really full freedom of propaganda and the immediate realization of a new democracy in the composition of the Soviets (new elections to them) and in their functioning would in themselves secure a peaceful forward movement of the revolution, *a peaceful outcome* of the party strike within the Soviets.

"Perhaps this is *already* impossible? Perhaps. But if there is even one chance in a hundred, the attempt at realizing such a possibility would still be worthwhile" (Lenin, *Collected Works,* vol. 25, p. 307).

In this case Lenin asked nothing more of the "civil and military chiefs" among the "ruling" petty-bourgeois democratic parties than that they take power and assure "really full freedom of propaganda." Returning to this question again on October 9, 1917, he wrote:

> "Our business is to help do everything possible to secure the 'last' chance for a peaceful development of the revolution, to help this by presenting our programme, by making clear its general, national character, its absolute harmony with the interests and demands of an enormous majority of the population" (Lenin, *Collected Works,* vol. 26, p. 60).

Thus, Lenin proposed to fight "the civil and military chiefs" in three different ways, according to the circumstances, on three different occasions—by "extermination," by "arrest" and by "peaceful propaganda." All were equally revolutionary. The occasions and the circumstances in each case were different.

Lenin took such variations into account and changed his proposals accordingly. He never made a strait jacket out of his tactical formulas. Neither should we—if we want to be genuine Leninists.

That "force is the midwife of every old society pregnant with the new"—this is an axiom known to every student of Marxism. It is wrong to entertain or disseminate illusions on this score, and we did not do so at the trial. But it is a great mistake to conclude from this that violence and the talk about violence serve the revolutionary vanguard advantageously at all times and under all conditions. On the contrary, peaceful conditions and democratic legal forms are most useful in the period when the party is still gathering its forces and when the main strength and resources, including the resources of violence are on the other side. Lenin remarked that Engels was "most correct" in "advocating the use of bourgeois legality" and saying to the

German ruling class in 1891: "Be the first to shoot, Messrs. Bourgeois!"

Our party, which must still strive to *get a hearing* from the as yet indifferent working class of America, has the least reason of all to emphasize or to "advocate" violence. This attitude is determined by the present stage of class development and relation of forces in the United States; not, as Munis so generously assumes, by our exaggerated concern for a "light sentence." As a matter of fact the question of violence was given ten times more proportionate mention in our testimony at the trial than it has been given in the propaganda columns of our press during the past ten years, including the voluminous contributions of Comrade Trotsky.

Expressing disdain for our repeated painstaking explanations "about who initiates the violence," and our "general tone" which, he says, "makes one feel embarrassed at times," Munis offers us "proud valor" as a substitute. Had we been gifted with this rare attribute we should have said, according to Munis: "The workers and farmers should respond to the daily violence of the bourgeoisie with majority and organized violence of the poor masses. We do not predict but rather we assure, we ask, we advocate temporary violence of the majority against the permanent organic violence of the reactionary minority."

We don't know much about "proud valor" and had no need of it; we did not appear at the trials as posturing actors but only as party militants with a practical political task to carry out. Naturally, it is a good thing for a revolutionary militant to have ordinary human courage enough to take those risks which are implicit in the struggle against capitalism. And we can add: He should also have enough prudence to avoid unnecessary sacrifices. The lack of either of these qualities can be a serious personal deficiency. But the possession of both, and in good working order at that, still does not suffice to answer the most important question confronting us at the trial; namely, what formulations, what tone, what emphasis on the question of violence could best serve our cause under the given conditions? The answer to the question must be political, not theatrical.

Lenin unquestionably burned with indignation and hatred for the oppressions of the people and knew about the violence of all kinds that is inseparable from a regime of class domination. Also, while it is quite impossible to speak of "valor" to say nothing of "proud valor," in connection with the unpretentious and matter-of-fact Lenin—such knightly grandiloquence would fit him as oddly as a silk hat—there is evidence that he had nerve enough to fill his post. Lenin was the most stiff-necked rebel in history. But his approach to the question of violence, as to every other question, was determined by political considerations. He did not by any means employ one universal formula and one kind of emphasis such as Munis prescribes for us. Indeed, he was far less "radical" in his formulations for the propaganda of the Bolshevik Party in the months, and even the weeks, directly preceding the victory than is Munis in his demands on our party which at the time of the trial could only be described properly as a small and isolated propaganda group.

It is most revealing to read how the great master of revolutionary strategy, returning to Russia after the March revolution, developed the work of *mobilizing the masses* around the Bolshevik Party by *means of propaganda.* The Bolshevik Party grew by leaps and bounds, but nevertheless remained a minority for many months. It should be instructive to any "violence" fanatic to see how Lenin, under these conditions, persistently tried to *shove the question of violence into the background* and to ward off a premature test of strength. Even as late as October 9, as we have seen, he was offering "to help do everything possible to secure the 'last' chance for a *peaceful development* of the revolution." When he finally called for action it was for *mass* action and there was no theatrical bluster about it. The Bolshevik Party, thanks to its preliminary propaganda work, had the mass force to carry the action through to victory.

On April 25 he protested in *Pravda* against "dark insinuations" of "Minister Nekrasov" about "the preaching of violence" by the Bolsheviks:

> "Mr. Minister, worthy member of the 'People's Freedom Party,' you are lying. It is Mr. Guchkov who preaches violence when he threatens to punish the soldiers for removing authorities. It is the *Russkaia Volia,* the pogrom newspaper of the pogrom 'republicans' and friendly to you that preaches violence.
>
> "The *Pravda* and its followers do not preach violence. On the contrary, they declare most clearly, precisely, and definitely, that our main work should at present be concentrated on *explaining* to the proletarian masses their proletarian problems, as distinguished from the problems of the petty bourgeoisie which has succumbed to chauvinist poison" (Lenin, *Collected Works,* vol. 24, p. 110–111).

On May 4 the Central Committee of the party adopted a resolution written by Lenin. The aim of this resolution was to restrain the Petrograd local leadership which was running ahead of events; to put the "responsibility" for any violence on the "Provisional Government and its supporters"; and to accuse the "capitalist minority" of reluctance "to submit to the will of the majority." Here are the two paragraphs from the resolution:

> "1. Party agitators and speakers must refute the despicable lies of the capitalist papers and of the papers supporting the capitalists to the effect that we threaten with civil war. This is a despicable lie, for at the present moment, when the capitalists and their government cannot and dare not use violence against the masses, when the mass of soldiers and workers freely expresses its will, freely elects and replaces all public officers,—at such a moment any thought of civil war is naive, senseless, monstrous; at such a moment there must be full compliance with the will of the majority of the population and free criticism of this will by the dissatisfied minority; should violence be resorted to, the responsibility will fall on the Provisional Government and its supporters.

"2. The government of the capitalists and its newspapers, by their noisy denunciation of the alleged civil war, are only trying to conceal the reluctance of the capitalists, who admittedly constitute an insignificant minority of the people, to submit to the will of the majority" (Lenin, *Collected Works,* vol. 24, p. 201).

Doesn't this sound surprisingly like "the lamentable dialogue about who initiates the violence" concerning which Munis so haughtily protests? Indeed, the similarity is not accidental. Our formulations did not fall from the sky. We had taken the trouble to read Lenin, not in order to memorize his words but to learn the essence of his methods of approaching and mobilizing the masses while the Bolsheviks remained in the minority.

On May 5 the Central Committee of the Bolshevik Party, fighting against enemy provocations on the one side and revolutionary impatience in the party ranks on the other, adopted another resolution on Lenin's motion. It is worth reading over ten times by any comrade who may be impressed by light-minded talk about "action" by a party which lacks the necessary mass support for action. The resolution says:

"The slogan, 'Down with the Provisional Government,' is at the present moment not sound, because such a slogan, unless there is a solid (i.e., a class conscious and organized) majority of the people on the side of the revolutionary proletariat, is either a mere phrase, or, objectively, reduces itself to encouraging efforts of an adventurous nature" (Lenin, *Collected Works,* vol. 24, pp. 210–11).

If these ideas are correct, and we believe they are, then it is certainly reasonable to conclude that the Socialist Workers Party in the United States has some long, hard days of propaganda work of *patiently explaining,* ahead of it. By such means it must secure a mass support before it can afford the luxury of much talk about action. Lenin drew these conclusions for the Bolshevik Party, and laid down precise instructions accordingly, only six months before it was to become the majority. The same resolution says in another paragraph:

"The slogans of the moment are: (1) *Elucidation* of the proletarian policy and proletarian method of terminating the war; (2) *criticism* of the petty-bourgeois policy of confidence in and agreement with the capitalist government; (3) *propaganda and agitation* from group to group, within each regiment, in each factory, particularly amongst the most backward masses, servants, unskilled labourers, etc., for it is mostly on them that the bourgeoisie tried to base itself during the days of the crisis; (4) *organisation, organisation and once more organisation* of the proletariat: in each factory, in each district in each block" (Lenin, *Collected Works,* vol. 24, p. 211; our emphasis).

On May 6, still hammering at irresponsible violence-mongers, the greatest leader of revolutionary action, who believed in first *"explaining"* and *"convincing"* and *"winning over the majority,"* wrote:

"Crises cannot be overcome by the violence of individuals against other individuals, by partial risings of small groups of armed people, by Blanquist attempts to 'seize power,' to 'arrest' the Provisional Government, etc.

"The slogan of the day is: Explain more carefully, more clearly, more broadly the proletarian policy, the proletarian method of terminating the war" (Lenin, *Collected Works,* vol. 24, p. 216).

Marxism, without a doubt, is the doctrine of revolutionary action. But it has nothing in common with "violence of individuals," "partial risings of small groups," or any other form of "action" wherein individuals or minorities attempt to substitute themselves for the masses. In other words Marxism is not anarchism or Blanquism; it wages irreconcilable war against such tendencies. The revolutionary action which Marxism contemplates is the action of the masses, of the proletarian majority, led by the vanguard party. But this action, and the party's leading role in it must be, and can only be, *prepared by propaganda*. That is the central lesson of the development of the Bolshevik Party after the March revolution and the eventual transformation of it slogans from propaganda to action. That was Lenin's method. It was less romantic than that of impatient people who dream of short cuts and miracles to be evoked by the magic word "action." But, in compensation, Lenin's method led to a mighty and victorious mass action in the end.

A party which lacks a mass base, which has yet to become widely known to the workers, must approach them along the lines of propaganda, of patient explanations, and pay no attention to impatient demands for "action" which it is unable to organize and for exaggerated emphasis on "violence" which, in the given conditions, can only react to its disadvantage. When one considers how persistently careful and even *cautious,* was Lenin's party to avoid provocation and cling to its formula of *peaceful propaganda* while it remained a minority, the merest suggestion that our party, at the present time, with its present strength, take a "bolder" course appears utterly fantastic, like a nightmare separated from living reality. Lenin wrote:

> "The government would like to see us make the first reckless step towards decisive action, as this would be to its advantage. It is exasperated because our party has advanced the slogan of peaceful demonstration. We must not cede one iota of our principles to the watchfully waiting petty bourgeoisie. The proletarian party would be guilty of the most grievous error if it shaped its policy on the basis of subjective desires where organisation is required. We cannot assert that the majority is with us; in this case our motto should be: caution, caution, caution" (Lenin, *Collected Works,* vol. 24, p. 237).

From the foregoing it should be clear that our disavowal of "responsibility" for violence in the testimony before the court at Minneapolis was not a special device invented by us "to reconcile the jury," as has been alleged; our formulation of the question, taken from Lenin, was designed to serve the political aims of our movement in the given situation. We did not, and had no need to, disregard legality and "advocate" violence as charged in the indictment.

But neither did we represent ourselves as pacifists or sow pacifist illusions. Far from it. We elucidated the question of violence and the socialist transformation of society in the same way that our great teachers, who organized a revolution, elucidated it. More than that we gave a sufficiently frank and precise justification of the defensive violence of the workers in the daily class struggle this side of the revolution. The court record bulges with proof that we had indeed advocated the organization of workers defense guards. The testimony goes further—and this is a not unimportant detail—and reveals that we translated the word into deed and took a hand in the actual organization and activities of defense guards and picket squads when concrete circumstance made such actions possible and feasible.

We are not pacifists. The world knows, and the prosecutor in our trial had no difficulty in proving once again, that the great Minneapolis strikes, led by the Trotskyists, were not free from violence and that the workers were not the only victims. We did not disavow the record or apologize for it. When the prosecutor, referring to one of the strike battles in which the workers came out victorious, demanded: "Is that Trotskyism demonstrating itself?" he received a forthright answer. The court record states:

"A: Well, I can give you my own opinion, that I am mighty proud of the fact that Trotskyism had some part in influencing the workers to protect themselves against that sort of violence.

"Q: Well, what kind of violence do you mean?

"A: This was what the deputies were organized for, to drive the workers off the street. They got a dose of their own medicine. I think the workers have a right to defend themselves. If that is treason, you can make the most of it."

With this testimony we said all that needs to be said on the question of violence in the daily class struggle, as in the previously quoted testimony we said enough about violence and the transition to socialism. If this method of presentation did not help the prosecutor, we can say again: That was not our duty. If it is objected that even in this example of the Minneapolis strike, dealing with an indubitable case of working-class violence, we insisted on its *defensive* nature, we can only reply: In real life the difference between careful defensive formulation and light-minded "calls for action" is usually, in the end result, the difference between real action and mere talk about it.

Our repeated insistence at the trial that we *prefer* a peaceful transition to socialism, and that we resort to violence only as a defensive measure, brings objection and ridicule from our critic. "Why not," says Munis—"why not ask forgiveness, besides, for seeing ourselves painfully obliged to employ violence against the bourgeoisie?" It is possible that others may regard our formulation as lacking in aggressiveness and militancy but, being more indulgent than Munis, pass it off as a legal euphemism, justifiable under the circumstances. To be sure, our formulation helped our position from a legal standpoint and we did not hesitate to emphasize it in this respect. Also, in our opinion, the declaration that we, the Trotskyists, prefer a peaceful change of society, is a good propaganda approach to the democratic-minded American workers. These two considerations are very important, but we are quite ready to agree that they would not justify the use of a false or hypocritical statement, or a statement contradicting principle.

We were guilty of no such dereliction. Our formula in this case also is the formula of the Marxist teachers. They not only insisted on the *desirability* of a peaceful change of society, but in certain exceptional circumstances, considered such a peaceful revolution possible. We, on our part, rejected any such prospect in the United States, but at the same time declared our preference for it and accused the ruling bourgeoisie as the instigators of violence. In this we were completely loyal to Marxist doctrine and tradition. On the witness stand at Minneapolis we mentioned the opinion of Marx and Engels in regard to

England in the 19th century. Here is the exact quotation from Engels:

> "Surely, at such a moment, the voice ought to be heard of a man whose whole theory is the result of a life-long study of the economic history and condition of England, and whom that study led to the conclusion that, at least in Europe, England is the only country where the inevitable social revolution might be effected entirely by peaceful and legal means. He certainly never forgot to add that he hardly expected the English ruling classes to submit, without a 'proslavery rebellion,' to this peaceful and legal revolution" (Engels, Preface to Marx's *Capital,* vol. I, Kerr Edition, p. 32).

We should have added that the conditions of England in Marx's time exist no more and therewith his calculation is out of date and no longer applicable. At any rate, we made this clear with regard to the United States.

In *Terrorism and Communism,* a book aimed from beginning to end at the bourgeois-democratic fetishism of Kautsky, Trotsky defended the violence of the proletarian revolution as a weapon *forced upon it* by the violence of the counter-revolutionary bourgeoisie; never did he renounce a preference for the peaceful way. In his introduction to the Second English Edition, published in England under the publishers' title, *In Defense of Terrorism,* he explains the position as follows:

> "From the Fabians we may hear it objected that the English proletariat have it quite in their own hands to come to power by way of Parliament, to carry through peacefully, within the law and step by step, all the changes called for in the capitalist system, and by so doing not only to make revolutionary terrorism needless, but also to dig the ground away under the feet of counter-revolutionary adventurers. An outlook such as this has at first sight a particular persuasiveness in the light of the Labour Party's very important successes in the elections—but only at first sight, and that a very superficial

one. The Fabian hope must, *I fear,* be held from the very beginning to be out of the question. *I say 'I fear,' since a peaceful, parliamentary change over to a new social structure would undoubtedly offer highly important advantages from the standpoint of the interests of culture, and therefore those of socialism.* But in politics nothing is more dangerous than to mistake what we wish for what is possible" (Trotsky, Introduction to Second English Edition of *In Defense of Terrorism,* p. v; our emphasis).

We tried to say the same thing at the trial in our own words and in our own way, suited to the circumstances. In this classic formulation of the question, the legal and propagandistic advantages of our "preference for a peaceful transition" fall into their proper place beside, and subordinate to, the most weighty considerations of all: "The interests of culture, and therefore those of socialism."

Trotsky, again, in his introduction to the book *on The Living Thoughts of Marx,* foretold a violent revolution for the United States, but he did not neglect to place the blame on the ruling class and express a different preference. Said Trotsky:

"It would be best, of course, to achieve this purpose in a peaceful, gradual democratic way. But the social order that has outlived itself never yields its place to its successor without resistance" (p. 33).

Lenin, as has been shown heretofore, denied the accusations of Bolshevik responsibility for violence so often that more than one critic of that revolutionary time, sick with radicalism and impatient for "action," might well have reproached him for the "euphemistic, sweetened character" of his statements and taunted him with the ironical query: "Why not ask forgiveness, besides?" However that may be, Lenin, preparing the greatest mass action in history by means of propaganda, insisted right up to the end that he preferred the peaceful road.

On October 9–10 he promised support to the Soviets "in every way" if they would but assume power and thus secure a peaceful development:

> "The proletariat will stop before no sacrifices to save the revolution, which is impossible without the programme set forth above. On the other hand, the proletariat would support the Soviets in every way if they were to make use of their last chance for securing a peaceful development of the revolution" (Lenin, *Collected Works,* vol. 26, p. 68).

In the same article he maintained that even at that late day the Soviets had the possibility—"probably their last chance"— to secure a peaceful development:

> "Having seized power, the Soviets could still at present—and this is probably their last chance—secure a peaceful development of the revolution, peaceful elections of the deputies by the people, a peaceful struggle of parties inside of the Soviets, a testing of the programmes of various parties in practice, a peaceful passing of power from one party to another" (Lenin, *Collected Works,* vol. 26, p. 67).

As late as September 29 he contended that in Russia, under the unique conditions which he cited, "an exceptional historic moment" a peaceful transformation was even *probable*:

> "The peaceful development of any revolution is, generally speaking, an extremely rare and difficult thing, for a revolution is the maximum sharpening of the sharpest class contradictions; but in a peasant country at a time when a union of the proletariat with the peasantry *can* give *peace* to the masses that are worn out by a most unjust and criminal war, when such a union can give the peasantry *all the land,* in such a country, at such an exceptional historic moment, a peaceful development of the revolution is *possible* and *probable* if all power passes to the Soviets.
>
>   Within the Soviets the struggle of parties for power may proceed peacefully, with the Soviets fully democratised, with 'petty thefts' and defrauding of democratic principles elimi-

nated—such as giving the soldiers one representative to every five hundred, while the workers have one representative to every thousand voters. In a democratic republic such petty thefts are doomed to disappear" (Lenin, *Collected Works,* vol. 26, pp. 36–37).

Trotsky, in his *History,* has explained this strategy of the Bolsheviks which was untainted by the fetishism of violence:

"The transfer of power to the soviets meant, in its immediate sense, a transfer of power to the Compromisers. That might have been accomplished peacefully, by way of a simple dismissal of the bourgeois government, which had survived only on the good will of the Compromisers and the relics of the confidence in them of the masses. The dictatorship of the workers and soldiers had been a fact ever since the 27th of February. But the workers and soldiers were not to the point necessary aware of that fact. They had confided the power to the Compromisers, who in their turn had passed it over to the bourgeoisie. The calculations of the Bolsheviks on a peaceful development of the revolution rested, not on the hope that the bourgeoisie would voluntarily turn over the power to the workers and soldiers, but that the workers and soldiers would in good season prevent the Compromisers from surrendering the power to the bourgeoisie.

"The concentration of the power in the soviets under a regime of soviet democracy, would have opened before the Bolsheviks a complete opportunity to become a majority in the soviet, and consequently to create a government on the basis of their program. For this end an armed insurrection would have been unnecessary. The interchange of power between parties could have been accomplished peacefully. All the efforts of the party from April to July had been directed towards making possible a peaceful development of the revolution through the soviet. 'Patiently explain'—that had been the key to the Bolshevik policy" (Trotsky, *History of the Russian Revolution,* vol. II, pp. 312–313).

These words of the two greatest leaders of Marxism in action should have an instructive value for all revolutionary militants. Lenin's sincere and earnest talk about a "peaceful development of the revolution"; his offer to "make compromises" to assure "the last chance" for it; Trotsky's summary statement that the "key to the Bolshevik policy" had been the simple prescription: "patiently explain"—in all this it is shown that Lenin and Trotsky were completely free from radical bombast about violence. But in return, they organized a victorious proletarian revolution.

And they had prepared so well that the transfer of power did indeed take place in Petrograd without any large-scale violence. We did not falsify the historical fact at the trial when we said there was "just a little scuffling, that's all." The violence came afterward, initiated by the "proslavery rebellion" which was eventually crushed by the mass force of the people led by the Bolshevik Party. These impressive facts give the explanations and formulas of Lenin and Trotsky a certain authority for those who want to be Marxists.

Comrade Munis is dissatisfied with our assertions at the trial that "we submit to the majority." The Oehlerites also are scornful of this declaration and represent it as some kind of capitulatory repudiation of our principles in order to impress the jury. All these assumptions are without foundation. Our "submission to the majority" was not first revealed at the trial. We said it before the trial and continue to repeat it after the trial. It is a correct statement of our position because it conforms both to reality and necessity. Moreover, our Marxist teachers said it before us; we learned it from them.

What else can we do but "submit to the majority" if we are Marxists, and not Blanquists or anarchist muddleheads? It is a timely occasion to probe into this question because we believe any ill-considered talk about some kind of mysterious "action," presumed to be open to us while we remain not only a minority, but a very small, numerically insignificant minority, can lead only to a dangerous disorientation of the party. An exposition of the Marxist position on this question can also be useful as an antidote for any remnants of the half-Blanquist tradition of the early years of the Comintern in America.

The pioneer communists in the United States (and not only here) heard of the Bolshevik victory in Russia long before they learned about the political method and propaganda techniques whereby the Bolsheviks gained the mass support which made the seizure of power possible. Their first impressions were undoubtedly colored by the capitalist press accounts which represented the revolution as a coup d'etat engineered by a small group. This distorted conception was epitomized by the title given to the American edition of Trotsky's classic pamphlet, *Terrorism and Communism,* which was published here by the party's publishing house in 1922 under the completely misleading title: *Dictatorship versus Democracy.* We took the "dictatorship," so to speak, and generously handed over to the bourgeoisie all claim to "democracy."

This was far too big a concession, perhaps pardonable in a young movement lacking adequate knowledge about the democratic essence of the Bolshevik program, but by far out of date today. The bourgeoisie have always tried to picture communism as a "criminal conspiracy" in order to alienate the workers who are profoundly democratic in their sentiments. That was the aim once again in the Minneapolis trial. It was our task at the trial to go out of our way to refute this misrepresentation and emphasize the democratic basis of our program; not in order to placate our enemies and persecutors, as is assumed, but in order to reveal the truth to our friends, the American workers.

We cannot eat our cake and have it too. We must either "submit" to the majority and confine ourselves to propaganda designed to win over the majority—or, we must seize power, more correctly, *try* to seize power and break the neck of the party, by minority "action."

Marxist authority is clear and conclusive in choosing between these alternatives. When we took our stand in court regarding "submission" to the majority we were not "folding our arms" and making "opportunistic" statements of "passivity in the face of the imperialist war," as we are accused. Nothing of the sort. The testimony states, repeatedly, and with sufficient emphasis, that, while "submitting to the majority"—that is, making no minority insurrections or putsches—we are organizing, speaking, writing, and "explaining"; in other words, carrying on *propaganda* with the object of winning over the *majority* to our program, which is the program of social revolution.

Neither were we simply trying to "make an honorable impression on the jury without taking into consideration that we should talk for the masses." To be sure we did not stupidly disregard the jury which held the fate of twenty-eight comrades, not to mention the legality of the party, in its hands. But we were speaking also, and *especially,* "for the masses." We testified primarily for publication. It was our deliberate aim to convince those who would read the testimony in printed form of the *truth* that the proletarian movement which we aspire to lead is a *democratic* movement, and not a "conspiracy," as the prosecutor and the whole of the capitalist press would picture it, and as loose talkers would unconsciously aid them to so picture it; not a scheme to transfer power from one clique to another, but a movement of the majority in the interest of the majority.

In addition, it may as well be said candidly that this testimony was also deliberately designed as an educational shock to such members and sympathizers of our movement as may still, at this late day, be dabbling with the idea of a shorter cut to socialism by some mysterious prescription for "action."

The Marxist authorities have all spoken in one voice on this question.

The *Communist Manifesto,* the first and the most fundamental statement of the principles of scientific socialism, defined the proletarian movement of emancipation, in contradistinction to all others in history, as follows:

"All previous historical movements were movements of minorities, or in the interest of minorities. The proletarian movement is the self-conscious, independent movement of the immense majority, in the interest of the immense majority" (Marx and Engels, *Communist Manifesto,* Pathfinder, p. 33)

The communist political method and strategy follow ineluctably from this basic premise. Nowhere and never have the authoritative representatives of Marxism formulated the question otherwise. The Marxists aim to make the social transformation *with* the majority and not *for* the majority. The irreconcilable struggle of Marx and Engels against the Blanquists revolved around this pivot.

In 1895, summing up the experience of fifty years, Engels wrote, in his Introduction to Marx's *Class Struggles in France:*

> "The time of surprise attacks, of revolutions carried through by small conscious minorities at the head of the unconscious masses, is past. Where it is a question of a complete transformation of the social organizations, the masses themselves must also be in it, must themselves already have grasped what is at stake, what they are going in for (with body and soul). The history of the last fifty years has taught us that" (Marx and Engels, *Collected Works,* vol. 27, p. 520).

The successors of Marx and Engels followed in their footsteps. The experiences of the Russian Revolution confirmed in life the basic premise of the founders of scientific socialism. It was precisely because Lenin and Trotsky had assimilated this concept into their flesh and blood that they knew how to concentrate their whole activity on *propaganda to win over the majority,* biding their time till they gained the majority, and resorting to "action" only when they felt assured of the support of the majority.

What did they do in the meantime? They *"submitted to the majority."* What else could they do? Lenin explained it a hundred times, precisely in those months and days when the Bolsheviks were consciously preparing the struggle for power. In his "April Theses" on "The Tasks of the Proletariat in the Present Revolution," published in *Pravda* on April 20, 1917, a few days after his return to Russia, Lenin wrote:

> "As long as we are in the minority we carry on the work of

criticising and exposing errors and at the same time advocate the necessity of transferring the entire power of state to the Soviets of Workers' Deputies, so that the masses may by experience overcome their mistakes" (Lenin, *Collcted Works,* vol. 24, p. 23).

A few days later, he returned to this question, explaining the reason for this attitude, the reason being that "we are not Blanquists, we are Marxists." On April 22 he wrote:

"In order to obtain the power of state the class conscious workers must win the majority to their side. *As long as* no violence is used against the masses, there is no other road to power. We are not Blanquists, we are not in favour of the seizure of power by a minority. We are Marxists, we stand for a proletarian class struggle against chauvinist defensism, phrases, and dependence on the bourgeoisie" (Lenin, *Collected Works,* vol. 24, p. 40).

Not once or twice, but repeatedly and almost continually, so that neither friend nor foe could possibly misunderstand him, in the months directly preceding the October Revolution, Lenin limited the Bolshevik task to the propaganda work of "criticizing," "exposing errors" and "advocating" in order to "win the majority to their side." This was not camouflage for the enemy but education for the workers' vanguard. He explained it theoretically as we, following him, tried to explain it in popular language at the trial.

Again, in April 1917, refuting the accusations of Plekhanov and others who accused the Bolsheviks of "anarchism, Blanquism, and so forth," Lenin once again explained the question, for the benefit, as he said, of "those who really want to think and learn." Into a few paragraphs he compresses a profound thesis which every member of the workers' vanguard ought to learn by heart. He wrote:

"I absolutely insured myself in my theses against skipping over the still existing peasant movement, or the petty-bourgeois movement in general, against the workers' government *playing* at the "seizure of power," against any kind of Blanquist adventurism; for I directly referred to the experience of the Paris Commune. And this experience, as we know, and as was shown in detail by Marx in 1871 and by Engels in 1891, absolutely excluded Blanquism, absolutely ensured the direct, immediate and unconditional rule of the *majority* and the activity of the masses, but only to the extent of the *conscious* and intelligent action of the majority itself.

"In the theses I definitely reduced the question to one of a *struggle for influence within* the Soviets of Workers', Agricultural Labourers', Soldiers', and Peasants' Deputies. In order to leave no trace of doubt in this respect I twice emphasized in the theses the necessity for patient and persistent 'explanatory' work 'adapted to the *practical needs of the masses.*'

"Ignorant persons or renegades from Marxism, such as Mr. Plekhanov, may cry anarchism, Blanquism, and so forth. But those who really want to think and learn cannot fail to understand that Blanquism means the seizure of power by a minority, whereas the Soviet of Workers', Agricultural Labourers', Soldiers' and Peasants' Deputies are admittedly the direct and immediate organisation of the *majority* of the people. Work confined to a struggle for influence *within* these Soviets cannot, absolutely *cannot,* blunder into the swamp of Blanquism. Nor can it blunder into the swamp of anarchism, for anarchism *denies the necessity for a state and for state power in the period of transition* from the rule of the bourgeoisie to the rule of the proletariat, whereas I, with a precision that excludes all possibility of misunderstanding, insist on the necessity for a state in this period, although, in accordance with Marx and the experience of the Paris Commune, not the usual parliamentary bourgeois state, but a state without a standing army, without a police opposed to the people, without an officialdom placed above the people" (Lenin, *Collected Works,* vol. 24, pp. 48–49).

Again explaining wherein "Marxism differs from Blanquism" —he obviously considered it absolutely necessary for the advanced workers to understand this so as to be sure of their ground at every step—he wrote in a letter to the Central Committee of the party on September 26–27, 1917:

> "To be successful, the uprising must be based not on a conspiracy, not on a party, but on the advanced class. This is the first point. The uprising must be based on the revolutionary upsurge of the people. This is the second point. The uprising must be based on the *crucial point* in the history of the maturing revolution, when the activity of the vanguard of the people is at its height, when the *vacillations* in the ranks of the enemies, and *in the ranks of the weak, half-hearted, undecided friends of the revolution are at their highest point.* This is the third point. It is in pointing out these three conditions as the way of approaching the question of an uprising, that Marxism differs from Blanquism" (Lenin, *Collected Works,* vol. 26, pp. 22–23).

Naturally, when Lenin, or any other Marxist, spoke of the necessity of the revolutionary party having the support of the majority he meant the real majority whose sentiments are ascertainable in various ways besides the ballot box of the bourgeois state. On the eve of the insurrection he wrote his devastating attack on Zinoviev and Kamenev, who opposed the insurrection on the ground, among other things, that "we do not enjoy a majority among the people, and in the absence of that condition insurrection is hopeless."

Lenin, in "A Letter to the Comrades," written on October 29–30, scornfully dismissed the authors of this statement as "either distorters of the truth or pedants who desire at all costs, without the slightest regard for the true circumstances of the revolution, to have a guarantee in advance that the Bolshevik Party throughout the country has received exactly one half the number of votes plus one." Nevertheless, he took pains to prove the Bolsheviks had the majority by "facts": "The elections of August 20 in Petrograd" . . . "The elections to the Borough Dumas in Moscow in September" . . . "The new elections to the Soviets" . . . "The majority of the Peasants'

Soviets" who had "expressed their opposition to the coalition"
. . . "The *mass* of the soldiers" . . . "Finally . . . the revolt of the peasantry." He concluded his argument on this point
by saying: "No, to doubt now that the majority of the people
are following and will follow the Bolsheviks is shameful vacillation."

Once again disavowing Blanquism, he wrote in his polemic
against Zinoviev and Kamenev:

"A military conspiracy is Blanquism *if* it is not organized by
the party of a definite class; *if* its organizers have not reckoned
with the political situation in general and the international situation in particular; *if* the party in question does not enjoy the
sympathy of the majority of the people, as proved by definite
facts . . ." (Lenin, *Collected Works,* vol. 26, pp. 196–97, 212).

On September 25–27 Lenin called upon the Bolshevik Party
to take power. In this famous letter, addressed "to the Central
Committee, the Petrograd and Moscow Committees of the Russian Social-Democratic Labor Party," Lenin, with the logic and
directness which characterized him, states his premise and his
conclusion in the first sentence:

"Having obtained a majority in the Soviets of Workers' and
Soldiers' Deputies of both capitals, the Bolsheviks can and must
take power into their hands."

He was not worried about a "formal" majority; "no revolution ever waits for *this*." But he was sure of the *real* majority.
He insisted upon the revolution "right now," as he expressed it,
not sooner and not later, because:

"The majority of the people is *with* us. This has been proven
by the long and difficult road from May 19 to August 12 and
September 25: the majority in the Soviets of the capitals is
the *result* of the people's progress *to our side.* The vacillation
of the Socialist-Revolutionaries and Mensheviks, and the
strengthening of internationalists among them, is proof of the
same thing" (Lenin, *Collected Works,* vol. 26, p. 19).

The prosecution at the Minneapolis trial attempted to con-
vict us, as charged in the indictment, of an actual "conspiracy

to overthrow the government by force and violence." We successfully refuted this accusation, and the indictment covering this point was rejected by the jury. The most effective element of our refutation of this absurd charge against our small party was our exposition of the democratic basis of the proletarian program, of the party's reliance on the majority to realize its program, and its corresponding obligation, while it remains in the minority, to "submit to the majority." In making this exposition we had a legal purpose, but not only a legal purpose, in mind. As with all the testimony, it was designed primarily to explain and simplify our views and aims to the workers who would be future readers of the published court record.

We also thought a restatement of the Marxist position in this respect would not be wasted on the members of our own movement, and might even be needed. The discussion which has arisen on this question only proves that we were more correct in this latter assumption than we realized at the time. Socialism is a democratic movement and its program, the program of the vanguard party, can be realized only with the support of the majority. The party's basic task, while it remains in the minority, is "propaganda to win over the majority." To state this was not capitulation to the prejudices of the jury; it is the teaching of Marx and Lenin, as has been shown in the foregoing references.

Our insistence at the trial that we undertake revolutionary action only with the support of the majority and not over their heads has brought a criticism also in connection with our attitude toward war, but this criticism is no more valid than the others and has no more right to appeal to the authority of Lenin.

Comrade Munis quotes with sharp disapproval the following answer to a hypothetical question concerning what our attitude would be in the event of the United States entering the war (this was before the declaration of war):

"A decision has been made, and is accepted by the majority of the people, to go to war. Our comrades have to comply with that."

Munis widens the gap between his understanding of revolutionary policy and ours by strongly objecting to this, as it appears to us, obviously correct and necessary statement. He says:

"In the first place, the decision to go to war has not 'been made and accepted by a majority of the people.' This statement can be criticized very strongly, a statement that we would censure very energetically if it were made by a centrist. In place of accusing the government of leading the American people to the slaughter against the will of the majority, instead of accusing it emphatically before the masses and of demonstrating to them how the parliamentarian majority acts against the majority of the people, Cannon endorses Roosevelt's decision as if it really corresponded to the majority of the people."

This impassioned rhetoric contains neither logic, nor Leninism, nor understanding of my statement nor an answer to it. "In the first place," I didn't "*endorse* Roosevelt's decision, as if it really corresponded to the majority of the people." I said, "the decision (hypothetically) is *accepted* by a majority of the people," the decision which has been "made" by others, for obviously one does not "accept" a decision which he has made himself. But that is only a small point which illustrates that the testimony was carelessly read before it was even more carelessly criticized.*

In the essence of the matter, the majority do in fact *accept*

---

* From similar carelessness in reading the testimony, Munis blithely represents us as "asking the expulsion from the party of the militants who organize protests in the army," and of "disauthorizing agitation and protests in the army." On the contrary, we defended the right of such agitation and protests, as a not too hasty reading of the testimony will convince anyone who is interested. What we "disauthorize" is futile and suicidal individual acts of insubordination and obstruction by members of our small party, acts which could only isolate them from the soldier mass under the given conditions and operate against the aim of winning over the majority. That is not the same thing as "disauthorizing agitation and protests in the army."

and *support* either actively or passively, the "decision to go to war." This is an incontestable fact, as shown by the complete absence of mass opposition. It is this attitude of the majority which we have to contend with. The fact that the decision was *made* by others does not help us. It is the attitude of the masses toward the decision that we must contend with.

What can and what should we, as Leninists, do while the masses maintain their present attitude?—that is the question. To make our position clear it is necessary to complete the answer given in the testimony which Munis broke off in the middle. He stops with our statement that "our comrades have to comply" without adding the sentences which explain what is meant by "compliance." Here are the explanatory sentences:

"Insofar as they are eligible for the draft, they must accept that, along with the rest of their generation, and go and perform the duty imposed on them, *until such time as they convince the majority for a different policy.*"

When the quotation is restored in full text it begins to look somewhat different than Munis hastily pictured it. It is nothing more or less than a warning to individual workers of the vanguard, who may be drafted, to "go with the rest of their generation" and not waste their energy and militancy on individual resistance, refusal of military service, etc. Was this warning correct? And was it necessary? As to the correctness of the warning, from the standpoint of Leninism, it will suffice to give two authoritative quotations. The first is a representative extract from Lenin's writings during the First World War:

"The idea of refusing to serve in the army, of strikes against the war, etc., is mere foolishness, it is the miserable and cowardly dream of an unarmed struggle against an armed bourgeoisie, it is a weak yearning for the abolition of capitalism without a desperate civil war or a series of wars" (Lenin, *Collected Works,* vol. 21, p. 40).

The second quotation is from the fundamental theses, *War and the Fourth International:*

"If the proletariat should find it beyond its power to prevent war by means of revolution,—and this is the only means of preventing war,—the workers, together with the whole people will be forced *to participate in the army and in the war*" (Leon Trotsky, *Writings, 1933–34,* p. 327).

This truth is presumably known to all revolutionists. But it was not always known. During the First World War many of the best proletarian militants in the United States knew no other way to express their principled opposition to the imperialist war than by individual resistance to conscription, objection to and refusal of military service, etc. Much precious energy and courage were wasted that way. In testifying before the court, with a view to the publication of the testimony, we assumed that rank-and-file worker militants, to whom Lenin's tactics are as yet unknown, might read and be influenced by this warning to "accept" with the masses—"until such time as they convince the majority for a different policy." Our words were primarily directed to them.

We were not even dreaming either of "endorsing Roosevelt's decision" or of having to defend this ABC formulation within our own movement. We simply intended to say, in words and tone which we thought most efficacious from a propagandistic standpoint in the situation, what Lenin said in February 1915:

"What should the Belgian Socialists have done? Since they could not accomplish a social revolution together with the French, etc., *they had to submit to the majority of the nation* at the present moment and go to war . . . 'Citizens of Belgium! . . . We are in the minority; *I submit to you and go to war,* but even in the war I shall preach; I shall prepare the civil war of the proletariat of all countries because outside of it there is no salvation for the peasants and workers of Belgium and of other countries!'" (Lenin, *Collected Works,* vol. 21, p. 112; our emphasis.)

Lenin, you see, "submits to the majority." While he is in the minority, what does he do? He "preaches" and "prepares." If this policy "can be criticized very strongly," then let the criti-

cism be directed against Lenin. He is the author of the policy.
We learned from him.

Munis quotes a sentence in the testimony: "We would not
support the war in a political sense." Now, this single sentence,
even standing by itself, is perfectly correct. But Munis is greatly
dissatisfied with it.

"Why, then, equivocate so dangerously?" he asks. "I see no
other reason but that our comrades have committed the very
grave error of talking for a petty-bourgeois jury for more immediate present, not foreseeing the future struggles. Would it
not have been better to state: 'We submit to your war, American bourgeois, because the violence of your society imposes it
on us, the *material violence of your arms*. But the masses *will*
turn against you. From today on, our party is *with* the masses
in an irreconcilable struggle against your regime of oppression, misery and butchery. Therefore we will fight against your
war with *all means*. (Our emphasis.)

This agitational substitute for the position we elucidated at
the trial is false from beginning to end, as we shall demonstrate.

The testimony explains what we mean by "political opposition":

"A: By that we mean that we do not give any support to
any imperialist war. We do not vote for it; we do not vote for
any person that promotes it; we do not speak for it; we do
not write for it. We are in opposition to it."

A declaration of war by the United States government would
not change our position:

"Q: If the United States should enter into the European conflict, what form would the opposition of the party take to the
war?

"A: We would maintain our position.

"Q: And that is what?

"A: That is, we would not become supporters of the war, even
after the war was declared. That is, we would remain an opposition political party on the war question, as on others.

"Q: You would not support the war?

"A: That is what I mean, we would not support the war, in a political sense."

Under cross-examination by the prosecuting attorney the position was made more emphatic and precise:

"Q: And you will seek to utilize war, during the war, to destroy the present form of government, will you not?

"A: Well, that is no secret, that we want to change this form of government.

"Q: And you look forward, do you not, to the forthcoming war as the time when you may be able to accomplish that?

"A: Yes, I think the forthcoming war will unquestionably weaken the imperialist governments in all countries.

"Q: You said, I believe, that you will not support the war? You do not believe in national defense at all, do you?

"A: Not in imperialist countries, no.

"Q: I am speaking of this country.

"A: I believe 100 per cent in defending this country by our own means, but I do not believe in defending the imperialist governments of the world—

"Q: I am speaking about the government of the United States as it is now constitutionally constituted. You do not believe in defending that, do you?

"A: Not in a political sense, no.

"Q: You do not believe in defending it in any sense, do you?

"A: I explained the other day, that if the majority of the people decide on war, and participate in the war, our people and the people under our influence will also participate in the war. We do not sabotage the war, we do not obstruct it, but we continue to propagate our ideas, calling for a cessation of the war and calling for a change in government."

When Mr. Schweinhaut, pursuing the question to the very end, introduced the summary paragraph of *the War Manifesto of the Fourth International,* he was answered by an affirmation of that document which was completely devoid of any "ambiguity" or "inexactness":

"Q: Now, on June 29, 1940, the *Socialist Appeal* published this from the report of the *Manifesto of the Fourth International:*

'Independently of the course of the war, we fulfill our basic task: We explain to the workers the irreconcilability between their interests and the interest of blood-thirsty capitalism; we mobilize the toilers against imperialism; we propagate the unity of the workers in all warring and neutral countries; we call for the fraternization of workers and soldiers within each country, and of soldiers with soldiers on the opposite side of the battle-front; we mobilize the women and youth against the war; we carry on constant, persistent, tireless preparation of the revolution—in the factories, in the mills, in the villages, in the barracks, at the front and in the fleet'. You want the soldiers to do that, don't you?

"A: Yes, I think that is a summation of the idea, for the soldiers and everybody to do that. That is the way to put an end to this slaughter."

In the face of these quotations from the court record one is reasonably entitled to ask: What does Comrade Munis want of us? What more needs to be said before the capitalist court, or in a popular propagandistic exposition anywhere? Neither Lenin or Trotsky, to judge from their own writings, would demand more of our party.

Trotsky, who was an internationalist to his heart's core, explained that a socialist party, which was in the minority at the outbreak of the First World War, was required to and *could only,* take up a position of *political opposition* until such time as "the change in the feeling of the working masses came about." That is the way he expounded the problem in *War and the International.* This book, written during the First World War and published in the United States under the publisher's title, *The Bolsheviki and World Peace,* is one of the classics upon which our movement has been raised and educated. Trotsky wrote:

"The advance guard of the Social Democracy feels it is in the minority; its organizations, in order to complete the organization of the army, are wrecked. Under such conditions there can be no thought of a revolutionary move on the part of the

Party. And all this is quite independent of whether the people look upon a particular war with favor or disfavor. In spite of the colonial character of the Russo-Japanese war and its unpopularity in Russia, the first half year of it nearly smothered the revolutionary movement. Consequently it is quite clear that, with the best intentions in the world, the Socialist parties cannot pledge themselves to obstructionist action at the time of mobilization, at a time, that is, when Socialism is more than ever politically isolated.

"And therefore there is nothing particularly unexpected or discouraging in the fact that the working-class parties did not oppose military mobilization with their own revolutionary mobilization. Had the Socialists limited themselves to expressing condemnation of the present War, had they declined all responsibility for it and refused the vote of confidence in their governments as well as the vote for the war credits, they would have done their duty at the time. They would have taken up a position of waiting, the oppositional character of which would have been perfectly clear to the government as well as to the people. Further action would have been determined by the march of events and by those changes which the events of a war must produce on the people's consciousness. The ties binding the International together would have been preserved, the banner of Socialism would have been unstained. Although weakened for the moment, the Social Democracy would have preserved a free hand for a decisive interference in affairs as soon as the change in the feelings of the working masses came about" (*The Bolsheviki and World Peace,* pp. 175–177).

The same idea was explained over again by Trotsky twenty-two years later in his testimony before the Dewey Commission in 1937. He still prescribes "political opposition" as a revolutionary method. At that time France had a military alliance with the Soviet Union and he was asked the hypothetical question by Stolberg:

"You are a responsible revolutionary figure. Russia and

> France already have a military alliance. Suppose an interna-
> tional war breaks out . . . What would you say to the
> French working class in reference to the defense of the Soviet
> Union? 'Change the French bourgeois government,' would
> you say?"

Trotsky's answer is especially interesting to us, since the
United States today stands in the position of France of 1937 in
relation to the Soviet Union, and the hypothetical war has become a reality:

"This question is more or less answered in the theses, 'The
War and the Fourth International,' in this sense: In France I
would remain in opposition to the Government and would develop systematically this opposition. In Germany I would do
anything I could to sabotage the war machinery. They are two
different things. In Germany and in Japan, I would apply military methods as far as I am able to fight, oppose, and injure
the machinery, the military machinery of Japan, to disorganize
it, both in Germany and Japan. In France, it is political opposition against the bourgeoisie, and the preparation of the proletarian revolution. Both are revolutionary methods. But in Germany and Japan I have as my immediate aim the disorganization of the whole machinery. In France, I have the aim of the
proletarian revolution" (*The Case of Leon Trotsky,* pp. 289–290).

In his "April Theses," which is a sufficiently authoritative document, since it was the program for the revolutionary struggle
of the Bolsheviks in Russia under conditions of war, Lenin
thought it enough, in dealing with the question of war and the
government, to say: "not the slightest concession must be made
to 'revolutionary defensism'"; "No support must be given to
the Provisional Government" because it is "a government of
capitalists"; power must be transferred to the Soviet; and then
to add:

"In view of the undoubted honesty of the mass of the rank-
and-file believers in revolutionary defensism, who accept the
war as a necessity only and not as a means of conquest; in view
of the fact that they are being deceived by the bourgeoisie, it is

necessary thoroughly, persistently and patiently to explain their error to them" (Lenin, *Collected Works,* vol. 21, pp. 21–22).

Political opposition ("No support to the Provisional Government") and *propaganda* ("patiently explain")—these are the weapons with which Lenin and Trotsky prepared and finally carried through the proletarian revolution. They will suffice for us too. Our propagandistic explanations of our war policy in the Minneapolis courtroom are neither "opportunistic" nor "equivocal." They contain the essence of the teachings and practice of Lenin and Trotsky.

The alternative formulas of Comrade Munis, however, contain one error after another. According to him, we should have said:

"We submit to your war, American bourgeois, because the violence of your society imposes it on us, the material violence of your arms."

That is not correct. If that were so we would have no right to condemn acts of individual resistance. When militant workers are put in fascist prisons and concentration camps because of their socialist opinions and activities they submit, but only through compulsion, to "the material violence of arms." Consequently, individuals or small groups are encouraged and aided to "desert," to make their escape whenever a favorable opportunity presents itself, without waiting for and without even consulting the majority of the other prisoners in regard to the action. The revolutionary movement gains by such individual "desertions" because they can restore the prisoner to revolutionary effectiveness which is largely shut off in prison. Trotsky, for example, twice "deserted" from Siberia without incurring any criticism from the revolutionists.

Compulsory military service in war is an entirely different matter. In this case we submit primarily *to the majority of the workers* who accept and support the war either actively or passively. Since we cannot achieve our socialist aims without the majority we must go with them, share their hardships and hazards, and win them over to our side by propaganda on the basis of common experiences. To accept military service under such circumstances is a revolutionary necessity. Individual resistance, objection, desertion, etc. in this case—directly contrary to that of prisoners escaping from "the violence of arms"—constitute desertion of class duty. The party, which applauds and aids the escaping prisoner, condemns draft dodgers and deserters. The escaped prisoner frees himself to resume revolutionary work. The individual deserter from the military service cuts himself off from the mass who have to make the revolution and thereby destroys his value.

"From today on," Munis would have us say, "our party is with the masses in an irreconcilable struggle against your regime of oppression, misery and butchery. Therefore we will fight against your war with all means."

The regime of the bourgeoisie is here justly described. The rest of it is incorrect and contradictory; it "skips a stage" in the evolution of the attitude of the masses toward the war, and precisely that stage which must be the point of departure for our propaganda—*the present stage*. To say to the bourgeoisie, "The masses *will* turn against you" in the future, means only that they have not yet done so. It cannot logically be followed by the assertion, "from *today* on, our party is *with the masses* in an irreconcilable struggle, etc."

The masses *today,* thanks to all kinds of compulsions and deceptions, and the perfidious role of the labor bureaucracy and the renegade socialists and Stalinists, are accepting and supporting the war, that is, they are acting *with the bourgeoisie* and not with us. The problem for our party is, first, to understand this primary fact; second, to take up a position of "*political opposition*"; and then, on that basis, to seek an approach to the honestly patriotic workers and try to win them away from the bourgeoisie and over to our side by means of *propaganda*. That is the only "action" that is open to us, as a small minority, at the present time.

It is also incorrect to say "we will fight against your war with *all* means." While we are in the minority we fight with the Marxist weapons of political opposition, criticism and propaganda for a workers' program and a workers' government. We reject the pacifist "means" of abstention, the anarchist "means" of individual sabotage and the Blanquist "means" of minority insurrection, the putsch.

It would appear that Munis' erroneous explanation of the primary reason why a minority revolutionary party "submits" to the war, his tendency to skip a stage in the workers' development and his lack of precision in speaking of the struggle against the war by "all means"—these errors lead him to slide over to equally loose and ill-considered formulations as to those means of struggle which are open, and advantageous, to the minority party of revolutionary socialism.

The everlasting talk about "action," as if a small minority party has at its disposal, besides its propaganda—its "explanations"—some other weapons vaguely described as "actions" but not explicitly defined, can only confuse and becloud the question and leave the door open for sentiments of an anarchistic and Blanquist nature. We, following all the Marxist teachers, thought it necessary to exclude such conceptions in order to safeguard the party from the danger of condemning itself to futility and destruction before it gets a good start on its real task at this time: to *explain* to the masses and win over the majority.

That is why we utilized the forum of the trial to speak so explicitly about our rejection of sabotage. That is why we denied all accusations in this respect so emphatically. Not—with Munis' permission—for lack of "valor," but because, as Marxists, we do not believe in sabotage, terrorism, or any other device which substitutes the actions of individuals or small groups for the action of the masses.

There can be no two positions on this question. Marxist authorities are universal on one side—against sabotage as an independent means of revolutionary struggle. This "weapon" belongs in the arsenal of anarchism.

Sabotage was once the fashion in this country—in the politically primitive days before the First World War. Imported from France where it was advertised as a miraculous remedy by the anarchists and anarcho-syndicalists, sabotage was taken up by the IWW, the left socialists, and the radical intellectuals, who in those days had a decidedly anarchistic hue. It seemed for a time to offer a wonderful short cut to victory for a movement which wasn't doing so well with the humdrum job of educating and organizing the workers for mass action.

The consequences of this anarchistic folly were disastrous for the IWW. The advocacy of sabotage only repelled the masses and left the IWW members in a legally indefensible position. To avoid complete alienation from the workers, and for sheer self-preservation of the organization in the face of prosecutions during the war, the IWW was compelled to drop the "weapon" of sabotage overboard with the most unseemly haste.

Those who have memories of this unhappy experience, especially those who, as participants in the American syndicalist movement burned their fingers on this hot poker, will be least of all inclined to play with the idea of sabotage again. Sabotage is not the slogan of proletarian power and confidence but of petty-bourgeois futility and despair.

The fundamental theses, *War and the Fourth International.* state categorically:

"Individualistic and anarchistic slogans of refusal to undergo military service, passive resistance, desertion, sabotage are *in basic contradiction* to the methods of the proletarian revolution" (Trotsky, *Writings, 1933–34,* p. 327; our emphasis).

Lenin wrote:

"Not the *sabotaging* of the war, not undertaking sporadic individual acts in this direction, but the conducting of *mass propaganda* (and not only among 'civilians') that leads to the transformation of the war into a civil war. . . . *We do not sabotage the war,* but we struggle against chauvinism . . ." (Lenin, *Collected Works,* vol. 28, p. 74; our emphasis).

Munis is especially indignant at our rejection of sabotage in the testimony, but he is wrong in his criticism and wrong even, it would appear, in his understanding of the question:

"The defendants," he says, "saw themselves forced to condemn sabotage in general, as though it dealt with something criminal."

Again:

"For moments there is evidence that the defendants really consider sabotage a crime. If I am not mistaken—and I hope I am—this is a dangerous moral predisposition."

To that we can only answer with the French expression: "It is worse than a crime—it is a blunder." As to the "moral" aspect of the question—that does not exist for us. Our considerations in this respect are exclusively political.

Of course, if one wants to discard precision of definitions and dump everything into one pot loosely described as "actions," disregarding proportion, circumstance, and the relation between actions which are *primary* and *fundamental* and those which are *subordinate* and *auxiliary*—in that case we can argue endlessly in a closed circle. But Marxism abhors vagueness of expression; it calls things by their right names—precisely.

Sabotage, to us, means individual acts of obstruction and destruction, substituted for mass action. That is the way Marxism defines it and, thereby, condemns it. Similarly, individual terrorism. But it is necessary to understand that such actions have one quality when employed as *substitutes* for mass action and another quality when subordinated to and absorbed by mass action. Marxism is opposed to terrorist assassinations, for example, but not to wars of liberation waged by the oppressed masses, even though wars entail some killing of obnoxious individuals. So, also, with acts of obstruction and destruction as *part of* and *subordinate* to wars waged by the masses, not as substitutes for them. "Terrorism" and "sabotage" are then no longer the same things. Everything changes, including the attitude of Marxists, according to what is *dominant* and what is *subordinate* in the circumstances.

Thus, if it is argued that Trotsky, in his answer to Stolberg, asked for sabotage of the military machinery in Germany and Japan, it must be pointed out that his proposal was made only in the event of war against the Soviet Union. Then sabotage in Germany and Japan would be not an independent revolutionary action but a secondary military measure of support to the mass action of the Red Army. Trotsky never asked for sabotage as a means of overthrowing a fascist or any other type of bourgeois regime from within.

Comrade Munis seems to invest sabotage with a virtue in its own right. We, on the other hand, admit "sabotage" only as a minor auxiliary factor in mass actions; that is, when it is no longer sabotage in the proper sense of the term. The difference is quite fundamental.

Munis writes: "I believe that sabotage is a method for tactical use whose application *at certain moments* can be productive of contrary effects to what is intended" (our emphasis).

This is putting the question upside down. Sabotage produces "contrary effects," not once in a while but always, when it is employed by itself as a substitute for mass action; like all anarchistic methods it tends to disorganize and demoralize the mass movement which alone can bring us to socialism through the proletarian revolution. Munis' formulation, contrasted to that of Trotsky in his article, "Learn to Think," shows a great difference of conception. Trotsky wrote:

"The proletarian party does not resort to artificial methods, such as burning warehouses, setting off bombs, wrecking trains, etc., in order to bring about the defeat of its own government. Even if it were successful on this road, the military defeat would not at all lead to revolutionary success, a success which can be assured only by the independent movement of the proletariat. . . .

"The methods of struggle change, of course, when the struggle enters the openly revolutionary phase. Civil war is a war, and in this aspect has its particular laws. In civil war, bombing of warehouses, wrecking of trains and all other forms of military 'sabotage' are inevitable. Their appropriateness is decided by purely military considerations—civil war continues revolutionary politics but by other, precisely military, means" (Trotsky, *Writings, 1937–38,* pp. 333–34).

Sabotage is admissible as a weapon of the proletarian movement only "in quotation marks" as elucidated by Trotsky. That is, when, strictly speaking, it is no longer sabotage, but a minor military measure supplementing mass action. Whoever speaks of sabotage in any other framework does not speak the language of Marxism.

In general, it may be said that the source of all the criticism of our expositions at the Minneapolis trial is to be found in the apparent rejection of defensive formulations, and in counterposing "offensive action" to them. But the essence of the whole question consists in this, that defensive formulations prepare and help to create genuine mass actions, while "calls to action," not so prepared, usually echo in the void. It is not by accident that those revolutionists who understand this are precisely the ones who have shown the capacity to organize actions when the conditions for them are present. The ultraleft sectarians, meantime, who do not understand the best mechanism for the organization of actions—that is, precisely, defensive formulations—always remain alone and isolated with their impatient slogans and their self-imagined intransigence.

Our critics explain our resort to defensive formulations by the theory that our strategy in court was determined above all by concern to obtain light sentences. "Our comrades . . . try to make an honorable impression on the jury without taking into consideration that they should talk for the masses." We seem to "have one policy for the masses and another for appearances before a bourgeois judge."

However, this appraisal of the motives of the defendants, which falls short of flattery, is somewhat contradicted by the fact that we immediately published the testimony in our press and then republished it in thousands of copies in pamphlet form, "for the masses." We do not deny anyone the right to his opinion as to the moral content of our conduct at the trial, and we do not intend even to debate the question on that ground. In this domain "actions speak louder than words." But we shall attempt a political exposition, basing ourselves on Marxist authority, of the role of defensive formulations in the organization of proletarian mass action.

Also, defensive formulations are an indispensable medium for teaching the masses, who will not be convinced by theory but only by their own experience and propaganda related thereto. This experience of the masses proceeds in the main along the line of defensive actions. That is why defensive formulations are most easily comprehensible and represent the best approach of the revolutionary Marxists to the masses. Finally, it is a tactical and legal consideration of no small importance in a bourgeois-democratic country that defensive formulas partially disarm the class enemy; or in any case, make their attacks more difficult and costly. Why should such advantages be thrown away?

Defensive formulations retain their efficiency in all actions involving masses, from the most elementary economic strikes to the open struggle for power. Those who aspire to organize action ought to know this.

American economic strikes have been explosively violent, and the violence has not all been on one side. The instinctive militancy of the workers, as revealed in these strikes, would indicate that when the time comes for grandiose revolutionary actions, these same workers will remain true to their tradition and not be paralyzed by Quakerism.

Every strike leader worth his salt knows, however, that strikers are not mobilized and sent into action against strikebreakers, thugs and law-breaking cops by lecturing them on the virtues of violence and "calling" them to take the "offensive." The workers, militant and courageous as they may be, prefer victory by peaceful means; and in this they only show good sense. In addition strikers, at the beginning, almost invariably entertain illusions about the impartiality of the public authorities and tend to assume that they, as well as the bosses and their hirelings, will respect the rights of the strikers and the justice of their cause.

They need experience, which as a rule is soon forthcoming, to change their attitude and move them to militant action. They need also some assurance that legal right is on their side. Strike leaders who seek not self-expression but victory in the strike, who understand that it can be won only by means of mass solidarity and mass action, must take these illusions and sentiments of the workers into account as the point of departure.

Strike leaders can in no case begin with loose-mouthed "calls" for violent offensive action by the strikers. The first task is to *explain* the implacable nature of the struggle in which the self-interest of the bosses excludes fair play, and the role of the public authorities as political servants of the bosses; the second task is to *warn* the workers to expect violent attacks; and the third task is to prepare and organize the workers to *defend themselves and their rights.* Along these lines, and as a rule only along these lines, the struggle can be consciously developed in tempo and scope. The most effective mass action of the strikers, as every experienced organizer of mass actions knows, is organized and carried out under *defensive slogans.*

Matters are no different when the workers' mass action ascends from the elementary field of the economic strike to the topmost peak of the class struggle—the open fight for political power. Here also the action proceeds under defensive slogans and, to a very large extent, also under cover of legality. Trotsky has demonstrated this so convincingly in his monumental *History of the Russian Revolution* that there remains no ground for serious debate in our ranks on the subject. To the student it should be sufficient to say: There is the book; go and read it. To the critic who imagines, without having thought the matter out, that defensive formulations signify squeamishness or hedging on principle, we say and we shall prove: That is the way the great Russian Revolution was organized and carried through to victory.

Here is the way Trotsky explains the question:

"The attacking side is almost always interested in seeming on the defensive. A revolutionary party is interested in legal coverings. The coming Congress of Soviets, although in essence a Soviet of revolution, was nevertheless for the whole popular mass indubitably endowed, if not with the whole sovereignty, at least with a good half of it. It was a question of one of the elements of a dual power making an insurrection against the other. Appealing to the Congress as the source of authority, the Military Revolutionary Committee accused the government in advance of preparing an attempt against the soviets. This accusation flowed logically from the whole situation. Insofar as the government did not intend to capitulate without a fight it could not help getting ready to defend itself. But by this very fact it became liable to the accusation of conspiracy against the highest organ of the workers, soldiers and peasants. In its struggle against the Congress of Soviets which was to overthrow Kerensky, the government lifted its hand against that source of power from which Kerensky had issued.

"It would be a serious mistake to regard all this as juridical hair-splitting of no interest to the people. On the contrary, it was in just this form that the fundamental facts of the revolution reflected themselves in the minds of the masses" (Trotsky, *History of the Russian Revolution,* vol. III, pp. 278–279; our emphasis).

Again:

"Although an insurrection can win only on the offensive, it develops better, the more it looks like self-defense. A piece of official sealing-wax on the door of the Bolshevik editorial rooms—as a military measure that is not much. But what a superb signal for battle!" (Trotsky, *History of the Russian Revolution,* vol. III, pp. 207–208.)

On the night of the victorious insurrection the Bolsheviks accused the official government as "conspirators" making an "assault" which had to be forcibly resisted:

"Telephonegrams to all districts and units of the garrison announced the event: 'The enemy of the people took the offensive during the night. The Military Revolutionary Committee is leading the resistance to the assault of the conspirators.' The conspirators—these were the institutions of the official government. From the pen of revolutionary conspirators this term came as a surprise, but it wholly corresponded to the situation and to the feelings of the masses" (Trotsky, *History of the Russian Revolution,* vol. III, p. 208).

This accusation was broadcast to the whole country. The insurrection was justified as a reply to the "offensive" of the enemy:

"The sailor Kurkov has remembered: 'We got word from Trotsky to broadcast . . . that the counter-revolution had taken the offensive.' Here too the defensive formulation concealed a summons to insurrection addressed to the whole country" (Trotsky, *History of the Russian Revolution,* vol. III, p. 208).

At every step, as the struggle unfolded and neared its climax, the Bolsheviks clung to their defensive formula, not as a petty deception but because that is the way the issue appeared to the workers and soldiers. Even at a caucus of Bolshevik delegates to the Soviet Congress, held on October 24, that is, the day of the insurrection, they still found it necessary to retain the "defensive envelope of the attack." Says Trotsky:

"There could be no talk of expounding before this caucus the whole plan of the insurrection. Whatever is said at a large meeting inevitably gets abroad. It was still impossible even to throw off the defensive envelope of the attack without creating confusion in the minds of certain units of the garrison. But it was necessary to make the delegates understand that a decisive struggle had already begun, and that it would remain only for the Congress to crown it" (Trotsky, *History of the Russian Revolution,* vol. III, p. 211).

On October 23, the day before the insurrection, an all-city conference of the Red Guard was held in Petrograd. The resolution adopted by the conference, says Trotsky:

". . . defined the Red Guard as 'an organization of the armed forces of the proletariat for the struggle against counterrevolution and the defense of the conquests of the revolution.' Observe this: that twenty-four hours before the insurrection the task was still defined in terms of defense and not attack" (Trotsky, *History of the Russian Revolution,* vol. III, p. 188).

Naturally, being Bolsheviks, their "defense" had nothing in common with the policy of folded arms. They were prepared for eventualities but they never gave up the advantage of "seeming on the defensive." Trotsky spoke at the caucus of Bolshevik delegates on the 24th:

> "Referring to recent articles of Lenin, Trotsky demonstrated that 'a conspiracy does not contradict the principles of Marxism,' if objective relations make an insurrection possible and inevitable. 'The physical barrier on the road to power must be overcome by a blow. . . .' However, up till now the policy of the Military Revolutionary Committee has not gone beyond the policy of self-defense. Of course this self-defense must be understood in a sufficiently broad sense. To assure the publication of the Bolshevik press with the help of armed forces, or to retain the Aurora in the waters of the Neva—'Comrades, is that not self-defense?—It is defense!' If the government intends to arrest us, we have machine guns on the roof of Smolny in preparation for such an event 'That also, comrades, is a measure of defense'" (Trotsky, *History of the Russian Revolution,* vol. III, pp. 211–212).

Trotsky painstakingly explains how the October Revolution was developed by defensive formulations from link to link over a period of thirteen or sixteen days during which "hundreds of thousands of workers and soldiers took direct action, defensive in form, but aggressive in essence." At the end of that time, the masses being fully mobilized, there remained "only a rather narrow problem"—the insurrection, the success of which was assured.

> "The October revolution can be correctly understood only if you do not limit your field of vision to its final link. During the last days of February the chess game of insurrection was played out from the first move to the last—that is to the surrender of the enemy. At the end of October the main part of the game was already in the past. And on the day of insurrection it remained to solve only a rather narrow

problem: mate in two moves. The period of revolution, therefore, must be considered to extend from the 9th of October, when the conflict about the garrison began, or from the 12th, when the resolution was passed to create a Military Revolutionary Committee. The enveloping maneuver extended over more than two weeks. The more decisive part of it lasted five to six days—from the birth of the Military Revolutionary Committee to the capture of the Winter Palace. During this whole period hundreds of thousands of workers and soldiers took direct action, defensive in form, but aggressive in essence. The final stage, when the insurrectionaries at last threw off the qualifications of the dual power with its dubious legality and defensive phraseology, occupied exactly twenty-four hours: from 2 o'clock on the night of the 25th to 2 o'clock on the night of the 26th" (Trotsky, *History of the Russian Revolution,* vol. III, p. 294).

Up to the decisive moment the Bolsheviks not only insisted on the defensive form of their actions; they also held onto Soviet legality "of which the masses were extremely jealous." It must have been a shock to Mr. Schweinhaut, the government prosecutor at the Minneapolis trial, when we defended the "legality" of the October Revolution. He, like many others, imagined that Bolsheviks disdainfully cast aside such trifles as legal justifications even when they are available. The prosecutor must have been still more discomfitted when we proved the legality of the revolution under cross-examination. And we were not dissimulating. Trotsky explained this question also in his refutation of Professor Pokrovsky who had attempted to make fun of the "legalistic" contentions of the Bolsheviks. Trotsky would not let such arguments pass even in the guise of jesting remarks. He answered:

"Professor Pokrovsky denies the very importance of the alternative: Soviet or party. Soldiers are no formalists, he laughs: they did not need a Congress of Soviets in order to overthrow Kerensky. With all its wit such a formulation leaves unexplained the problem: Why create soviets at all if the party is enough? 'It is interesting,' continues the professor, 'that nothing at all came of this aspiration to do everything almost legally, with soviet legality, and the power at the last moment was taken not by the Soviet, but by an obviously "illegal" organization created ad hoc.' Pokrovsky here cites the fact that Trotsky was compelled 'in the name of the Military Revolutionary Committee,' and not the Soviet, to declare the government of Kerensky non-existent. A most unexpected conclusion! The Military Revolutionary Committee was an elected organ of the Soviet. The leading role of the Committee in the overturn did not in any sense violate that soviet legality which the professor makes fun of but of which the masses were extremely jealous" (Trotsky, *History of the Russian Revolution,* vol. III, p. 288).

After these explanations of Trotsky about the defensive slogans whereby the Bolsheviks organized their victorious struggle for power it should not be necessary to say anything more on the subject. The method here acquires unimpeachable authority by virtue of the fact that it was not only expounded, but also successfully applied to the greatest revolution in history. In this light the defensive formulations employed by us in the Minneapolis trial, far from being repudiated, must be underscored more decisively. They are the right formulations for a propagandistic approach to the American workers. And they are the best methods for the mobilization of the workers for mass action throughout all stages of the development of the proletarian revolution in the United States.

New York, May 1942

Index

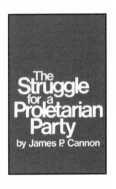

The History of American Trotskyism

Report of a participant

JAMES P. CANNON

"Trotskyism is not a new movement, a new doctrine, but the restoration, the revival of genuine Marxism as it was expounded and practiced in the Russian revolution and in the early days of the Communist International."

The story, told by a leading participant, of the effort in the decade from 1928 to 1938 to build a proletarian party in the United States modeled on the Bolshevik leadership of the Russian revolution. After a brief review of the early years of American communism, it focuses on the period following the expulsion from the Communist Party of those who supported the fight led by Russian revolutionary Leon Trotsky to continue the communist course of V.I. Lenin. In this book Cannon takes the story up to New Year's 1938, when the communist organization in the United States took the name Socialist Workers Party. $18.95

PATHFINDER

Capitalism's world disorder

Working-class politics at the Millennium

by Jack Barnes

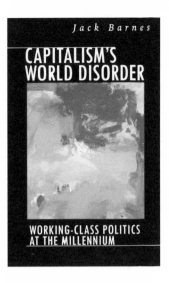

IT IS OFTEN SAID that great histor-ical crises are only resolved in struggle; that's true. But what is not said as often is that the odds — the probability of victory or of loss — are determined long be-fore these class battles them-selves break out. The odds depend on the self-confidence, political clarity, and previous combat experience of the cadres of disciplined proletarian organizations who are already among the fighters in the labor movement, and who know that what they do *beforehand* will be decisive when the working class moves toward revolutionary action.

Jack Barnes, April 1993

Five talks by the national secretary of the Socialist Workers Party. Jack Barnes discusses . . .

■ **Capitalist Deflation and Debt Slavery** ■ **Stalinism versus Communism** ■ **Buchananism: What It Is and How to Fight It** ■ **Washington Lets Yugoslavia Bleed** ■ **The 'Bell Curve': the Scandal of Class Privilege** ■ **Socialism and Lifetime Education** ■ **Cuba's Socialist Revolution** ■ **Youth and the Communist Movement** ■ **New Openings for Mass Work and the Struggle for a Proletarian Party**

$23.95

Also from Pathfinder

The Changing Face of U.S. Politics
Working-Class Politics and
the Trade Unions
JACK BARNES

A handbook for workers coming into the factories, mines, and mills, as they react to the uncertain life, ceaseless turmoil, and brutality of capitalism in the closing years of the twentieth century. It shows how millions of workers, as political resistance grows, will revolutionize themselves, their unions, and all of society. Also available in Spanish. $19.95

Out Now!
A Participant's Account of the Movement
in the United States against the Vietnam War
FRED HALSTEAD

The story of the anti–Vietnam War movement in the United States: how it refuted Washington's rationales for the war and mobilized opposition; the political fight for a course that could organize in action the maximum number of working people, GIs, and youth and help lead the growing international opposition; how the antiwar movement, gaining momentum from the fight for Black civil rights, helped force the U.S. government to bring the troops home, thus spurring struggles for social justice and changing the political face of the United States. $30.95

Labor's Giant Step
The First Twenty Years of the CIO: 1936–55
ART PREIS

The story of the explosive labor struggles and political battles in the 1930s that built the industrial unions. And how those unions became the vanguard of a mass social movement that began transforming U.S. society. $26.95

Cosmetics, Fashions, and the Exploitation of Women

JOSEPH HANSEN, EVELYN REED,
AND MARY-ALICE WATERS

How big business promotes cosmetics to generate profits and perpetuate the inferior status of women. In her introduction, Mary-Alice Waters explains how the entry of millions of women into the workforce during and after World War II irreversibly changed U.S. society and laid the basis for the advances women have won through struggle over the last three decades. $14.95

America's Revolutionary Heritage

Marxist Essays

EDITED BY GEORGE NOVACK

Essays on the struggle by Native Americans, the first American revolution, the Civil War, the rise of industrial capitalism, and the fight for women's suffrage. $21.95

The Leninist Strategy of Party Building

The Debate on Guerrilla Warfare in Latin America

JOSEPH HANSEN

In the 1960s and '70s, revolutionists in the Americas and throughout the world debated how to apply the lessons of the Cuban revolution to struggles elsewhere. Written with polemical clarity by a participant in that debate. $26.95

Lenin's Final Fight

Speeches and Writings, 1922–23

V.I. LENIN

In the early 1920s Lenin waged a political battle in the leadership of the Communist Party of the USSR to maintain the course that had enabled the workers and peasants to overthrow the old tsarist empire, carry out the first successful socialist revolution, and begin building a world communist movement. The issues posed in his political fight remain at the heart of world politics today. Several items appear in English for the first time. Also available in Spanish. $19.95

The Communist Manifesto

KARL MARX AND FREDERICK ENGELS

Founding document of the modern working-class movement, published in 1848. Explains how capitalism arose as a specific stage in the economic development of class society and how it will be superseded by socialism through worldwide revolutionary action by the working class. Also available in Spanish. $3.95

The History of the Russian Revolution

LEON TROTSKY

The social, economic, and political dynamics of the first socialist revolution, explained by one of the principal leaders of this victorious struggle which changed the course of history in the twentieth century. Unabridged edition, 3 vols. $35.95

On the Paris Commune

KARL MARX AND FREDERICK ENGELS

"Storming heaven," Marx wrote, the "proletariat for the first time held political power" in Paris for three months in 1871 and the international workers struggle "entered upon a new stage." Writings, letters, and speeches on the Paris Commune. $15.95

Imperialism: The Highest Stage of Capitalism

V.I. LENIN

"I trust that this pamphlet will help the reader to understand the fundamental economic question, that of the economic essence of imperialism," Lenin wrote in 1917. "For unless this is studied, it will be impossible to understand and appraise modern war and modern politics." Also available in Spanish. $3.95

The First Ten Years of American Communism

Report of a Participant

JAMES P. CANNON

An account of the early years of the U.S. communist movement, by one of its founding leaders. $19.95

The Teamster Series

Lessons from the Labor Battles of the 1930s

FARRELL DOBBS

Four books on the 1930s strikes and organizing drive that transformed the Teamsters union in Minnesota and much of the Midwest into a fighting industrial union movement. Written by a leader of the communist movement in the U.S. and organizer of the Teamsters union during the rise of the CIO, these are indispensable tools for advancing revolutionary politics, organization, and trade union strategy.

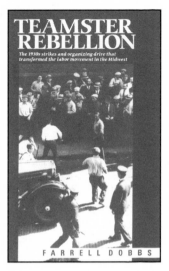

Teamster Rebellion $16.95
Teamster Power $17.95
Teamster Politics $17.95
Teamster Bureaucracy $18.95

Revolution and Counter-Revolution in Spain

FELIX MORROW

A contemporary account of the revolution and civil war in Spain in the 1930s in which the proletariat, betrayed by its Stalinist, social democratic, and anarchist leaderships, went down to defeat under the blows of an armed fascist movement. $17.95

Land or Death

The Peasant Struggle in Peru

HUGO BLANCO

The land occupations and struggles by peasants in the early 1960s, recounted by a central leader of the movement in Peru. $14.95

Malcolm X Speaks

Speeches from the last year of Malcolm X's life tracing the evolution of his views on racism, capitalism, socialism, political action, and more. Also available in Spanish. $17.95

Available from Pathfinder. Write for a free catalog.

The Cuban Revolution in World Politics

Episodes of the Cuban Revolutionary War, 1956–58

Ernesto Che Guevara

A firsthand account of the military campaigns and political events that culminated in the January 1959 popular insurrection that overthrew the U.S.-backed dictatorship in Cuba. With clarity and humor, Guevara describes his own political education. He explains how the struggle transformed the men and women of the Rebel Army and July 26 Movement led by Fidel Castro. And how these combatants forged a political leadership capable of guiding millions of workers and peasants to open the socialist revolution in the Americas. $23.95

In Defense of Socialism

Fidel Castro Speeches

Four Speeches on the 30th Anniversary of the Cuban Revolution, 1988–89
Not only is economic and social progress possible without the dog-eat-dog competition of capitalism, Castro argues, but socialism remains the only way forward for humanity. Also discusses Cuba's role in the struggle against the apartheid regime in southern Africa. $13.95

Fidel Castro's Political Strategy: From Moncada to Victory

Marta Harnecker

Featuring History Will Absolve Me *by Fidel Castro*
Traces the revolutionary course followed by Castro that culminated in the 1959 victory of the Rebel Army and July 26 Movement over the U.S.-backed Batista dictatorship. Also includes the full text of "History Will Absolve Me," Castro's reconstruction of his 1953 courtroom speech explaining the political and social goals of the revolution. $14.95

Che Guevara Speaks

Selected Speeches and Writings
"A faithful reflection of Che as he was, or, better, as he developed"— from the preface by Joseph Hansen. Includes works not available elsewhere in English. $14.95

New International
A MAGAZINE OF MARXIST POLITICS AND THEORY

New International no. 11
U.S. Imperialism Has Lost the Cold War *by Jack Barnes* • The Communist Strategy of Party Building Today *by Mary-Alice Waters* • Socialism: A Viable Option *by José Ramón Balaguer* • Young Socialists Manifesto • Ours Is the Epoch of World Revolution *by Jack Barnes and Mary-Alice Waters* $14.00

New International no. 10
Imperialism's March toward Fascism and War *by Jack Barnes* • What the 1987 Stock Market Crash Foretold • Defending Cuba, Defending Cuba's Socialist Revolution *by Mary-Alice Waters* • The Curve of Capitalist Development *by Leon Trotsky* $14.00

New International no. 9
The Triumph of the Nicaraguan Revolution • Washington's Contra War and the Challenge of Forging Proletarian Leadership • The Political Degeneration of the FSLN and the Demise of the Workers and Farmers Government. Documents and resolutions of the Socialist Workers Party by *Jack Barnes, Steve Clark,* and *Larry Seigle.* $14.00

New International no. 8

The Politics of Economics: Che Guevara and Marxist Continuity *by Steve Clark and Jack Barnes* • Che's Contribution to the Cuban Economy *by Carlos Rafael Rodríguez* • On the Concept of Value *and* The Meaning of Socialist Planning, two articles *by Ernesto Che Guevara* $10.00

New International no. 7

Opening Guns of World War III: Washington's Assault on Iraq *by Jack Barnes* • Communist Policy in Wartime as well as in Peacetime *by Mary-Alice Waters* • Lessons from the Iran-Iraq War *by Samad Sharif* $12.00

New International no. 6

The Second Assassination of Maurice Bishop *by Steve Clark* • Washington's 50-year Domestic Contra Operation *by Larry Seigle* • Land, Labor, and the Canadian Revolution *by Michel Dugré* • Renewal or Death: Cuba's Rectification Process, two speeches *by Fidel Castro* $15.00

New International no. 5

The Coming Revolution in South Africa *by Jack Barnes* • The Future Belongs to the Majority *by Oliver Tambo* • Why Cuban Volunteers Are in Angola, two speeches *by Fidel Castro* $9.00

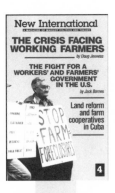

New International no. 4

The Fight for a Workers and Farmers Government in the United States *by Jack Barnes* • The Crisis Facing Working Farmers *by Doug Jenness* • Land Reform and Farm Cooperatives in Cuba, two speeches *by Fidel Castro* $12.00

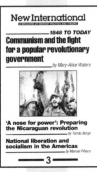

New International no. 3

Communism and the Fight for a Popular Revolutionary Government: 1848 to Today *by Mary-Alice Waters* • 'A Nose for Power': Preparing the Nicaraguan Revolution *by Tomás Borge* • National Liberation and Socialism in the Americas *by Manuel Piñeiro* $8.00

New International no. 2

The Aristocracy of Labor: Development of the Marxist Position *by Steve Clark* • The Working-Class Fight for Peace *by Brian Grogan* • The Social Roots of Opportunism *by Gregory Zinoviev* $8.00

New International no. 1

Their Trotsky and Ours: Communist Continuity Today *by Jack Barnes* • Lenin and the Colonial Question *by Carlos Rafael Rodríguez* • The 1916 Easter Rebellion in Ireland: Two Views *by V.I. Lenin and Leon Trotsky* $8.00

Distributed by Pathfinder

Many of the articles that appear in *New International* are also available in Spanish in *Nueva Internacional,* in French in *Nouvelle Internationale,* and in Swedish in *Ny International.*